EssaySnark's Strategies for the
2014-'15 MBA Application for
MIT SLOAN

EssaySnark's Strategies for the 2014-'15 MBA Application for MIT SLOAN

by EssaySnark®

Snarkolicious Press

First published August 1, 2012
2014 edition
version 4.0 July 9, 2014

Snarkolicious Press
P. O. Box 50021
Palo Alto, CA 94303

www.snarkoliciouspress.com

978 1 938098 28 4

© 2012-2014 by EssaySnark®

Cover image © Eric Isselée, used under license from Fotolia.com

All rights reserved. No part of this book may be reproduced or transmitted in any form or by any means, electronic or mechanical, including photocopying, recording, transcribing, or by an information storage system, without permission from the publisher. The essay questions are copyright MIT Sloan.

This publication is provided "as is", without warranty of any kind, either express or implied. The author and Snarkolicious Press assume no liability for errors or omissions in this publication or other documents which are referenced or linked to this publication. While we certainly hope that you will be successful in your quest for admission to an MBA program, we cannot offer any promises that you will be, whether or not you adopt the advice provided herein. In no event shall Snarkolicious Press or its authors, principals, subsidiaries, partners, or owners be liable for any special, incidental, indirect or consequential damages of any kind, or any damages whatsoever, arising out of or in conjunction with the use or performance of this information. Applicants to any graduate program or university should verify the school's policies, application requirements, processes, procedures, and other criteria. This publication could include technical or other inaccuracies or typographical errors. Changes are periodically added to the information herein; these changes will be incorporated into new editions of this publication. Thus, different versions or formats of this publication may include different information.

Look for other *SnarkStrategies Guides* (digital and paperback) at your favorite bookseller or on the EssaySnark blahg at essaysnark.com.

Follow EssaySnark on Twitter!

"By far the best proof is experience."

Sir Francis Bacon

About this *SnarkStrategies Guide*

You must be a quant. Or some kind of engineer. You're interested in MIT, so we figured...

Oh you're not? Isn't that the only type of person who they'll accept?

That's the common myth about MIT Sloan, and of course it's not true – but strength in quant does matter to MIT. And so do a whole slew of other things – different things, in fact, than what other schools are looking for.

This *SnarkStrategies Guide* will break them down for you. MIT is unique in many ways, and we're not able to distill all of it down in a 75-page book. You need to visit campus if you can. Get to know this place. Go beyond the gawd-awful torture devices of essay questions that the adcom is forcing you to deal with – and please remember that you won't be going to school with the adcom, so don't judge all of Sloan based on this application. Explore the school community, talk to some students. See if this is the right place for you, based on your own first-hand research and investigation into academics and opportunities. Then when it comes time to write your essays, you can turn to EssaySnark for help, after you're armed with your own opinions and information about their program.

What we cover in this *SnarkStrategies Guide* are all the many things that MIT does differently in their admissions process – the good, the bad and the ugly. For starters, as you are well aware, their essays are different. No career goals question. And that crazy recommendation "essay." What we can tell you now, right upfront, is that MIT has raised the bar in terms of what they are requiring applicants to present. You will need to have more stories of impact and achievement to present in this MIT app than you would ever be expected to cover in another school's.

The MIT interviews are totally different, too, in ways that we actually find to be positive. We'll offer our best understanding of the rationale behind these differences, to give you insights into their thinking, which will hopefully influence *your* thinking and help you present yourself in the strongest way possible.

We have to state right upfront though: We think MIT's essays this year truly suck. Their essays in 2013 were quite challenging and people really struggled with them, and not only did the Sloan adcom perpetuate that madness, but they added to it with this "recommendation" question. We can only guess that they thought they were being innovation, but c'mon. Did anyone at the adcom even try to sit down and sketch out what a good answer to that question might look like, or how it should be positioned? It's so lame that we even considered not publishing a 2014 essay guide for MIT. But that would be punishing you Brave Supplicants for the errors of a group of adults who should know better. And that would be just plain silly. The Sloan MBA experience is still a good one, however misguided those people in admissions might be.

The other heads-up we need to offer: At the time of this writing (early July), the Sloan admissions team has stated that they have no plans to travel to India this summer. They don't have any events listed there despite a full schedule of travel to host info sessions and alumni meet-and-greet events in places like Sao Paulo, Tokyo, and Istanbul. Why in heck would they not go to India?!? To EssaySnark, this seems like a bit of a slap in the face to all you Indians out there; we feel offended on your behalf. They know that they will get plenty of applications from that part of the candidate population, so they apparently have decided that they don't need to spend any money in hosting outreach and marketing events to that segment. Given how much they insist that applicants need to get to know them, in order to do a good job on the application, this seems to be a little unfair. We're not even seeing the standard Dubai stop on the calendar, which would at least be semi-accessible for many Indians. Talk about a diss.

Suffice it to say, MIT Sloan is just not on our list of favorite schools. They used to be, but that really has changed quite dramatically based on our experience with admissions in the past two years specifically. You can see some of our prior rants about their admissions team on the blahg. We even had to tone down some of our gushing about this school in the language used in this *Guide*. It's still a great education, but we are not fans of the policies in place and how things are being run in the front office.

We don't want to discourage you from applying; that would indeed be silly. As already stated, the admissions team is not the school. You're going to school with the students and the professors. You'll be part of the alumni community for life. Those are the elements you need to test for yourself, to see if you feel a sense of resonance with the people you encounter — *not* the admissions office.

We still try to serve you to the best of our abilities with information in this *SnarkStrategies Guides*, though just like with all the others, we will not tell you what to say in your essays — especially not these ones. There's a fair amount of interpretation required, and you have plenty of wiggle-room within which to operate as you map out your ideas. There are definitely some common errors that we will point out, in the hopes that you won't repeat the mistakes of others. But you will need to do the heavy lifting yourself.

Expect to dedicate a significant chunk of time to figuring out your strategy and writing your drafts. Yes, that's plural "drafts", as in, multiple. The MIT application is no joke. This process will take you some time. Using the advice in this *Guide* should make the overall process go more efficiently for you. Don't cut corners along the way. Hammer out your strategy and focus on details, and you'll be in good shape. Don't worry, we'll walk you through it.

If you find yourself stuck on anything, drop on over to our blahg at http://essaysnark.com and submit your question through the Contact page or post it as a comment on a post. If you have questions about our services, the team at gethelpnow@essaysnark.com can assist. You could even tweet us if it's a simple question and we'll see what we can do to help out.

Table of Contents

How MIT Is Different 1
    What you should not expect at Sloan 3
What's Changed, and What's Stayed the Same 4
What MIT Is Looking For 7
    Minimums and Standard Qualifications 9
The MIT Competency Scale 12
What's LGO and Should You Apply to It? 16
Important Nuances and Differences with an MIT Application 18
    When to apply 19
    Why don't they have a Round 3? 21
    What not to do 21
MIT MBA and Goals (or lack thereof) 23
MIT and Your Multi-School Strategy 26
    Which order should you do your apps in? 26
    Which order should you tackle the MIT components in? 27
Brainstorming and Prep Work for the Sloan Application 30
    Why do you want to go to MIT? 30
    An unfortunate reality 45
Essay 1: "The Mission" 47
    Your Most Significant Accomplishments 49
    What must be in Essay 1 51
    How to write Essay 1 52
Essay 2: Your Recommendation (Of Yourself) 54
    1. How long and in what capacity have you known the applicant? 57
    2. How does the applicant stand out from others in a similar capacity? 58
    3. Please give an example of the applicant's impact. 60
    4. Please give an example of how the applicant interacts with other people. 62
    5. Which of the applicant's personal or professional characteristics would you change? . 63
    6. Please tell us anything else you think we should know about this applicant. 64
    How to write Essay 2 65
    Before you get too far with Essays 1 and 2 66
Optional Answer 68
Resume 70
The MIT Interview 71
    Logistics 72
What to Do Next 74

How MIT Is Different

Hopefully you've done enough first-hand research into what Sloan is about that you already know how they're unique. If you haven't visited campus, maybe you have plans to do that at some point in the very near future. Before trying to write your essays is best if you can pull it off. If you do your homework, you have a much better chance of getting into MIT – and if you bother to visit, you're almost undoubtedly going to come away incredibly excited by the opportunity.

As we already alluded to in the intro, there are differences in how MIT handles admissions. Like other schools, MIT uses a holistic evaluation to assess its candidates, however MIT treats the "evaluation" part as a true science. Not too surprising, given that they focus on rational analysis as a main precept in their MBA education. If you're weaker on the quant side, be prepared to demonstrate to the adcom how you can hack it at this school – and be prepared to take some pre-MBA courses like microeconomics or statistics if you never had them before.

MIT does not care who you are. Young or old, whatever background you come from, they'll give you a fair shot at getting in – provided you demonstrate evidence of the way you operate, of how you think, of how you get results, in concrete terms through your application. That the gist of what needs to be in all the recommendations – not only in the one you will write about yourself, but the two others that you will ask people to submit on your behalf. Sloan will draw conclusions from those. They want to know literally what you've done before, in order to understand your strengths and skills.

The MIT admissions process is about *judging your actions* to determine if you're the kind of person who will thrive in the environment they offer. (This means that you cannot be *fudging your actions* when you write about what you've done – you need to bring your best descriptions of what you've really done.) MIT created a methodology for evaluating candidates in the most objective way possible. The bulk of this *Strategy Guide* is about sharing what we know on this methodology, so that you can understand how they'll look at your app. As with all our *Guides* we'll be doing our best to give you the perspective of the admissions committee (even when we don't agree with it) so you can bring an understanding of their priorities into your essay-writing experience.

MIT's website has quite a bit of useful information – though it's also been known to contradict itself. This is a big problem at this school, actually: You might get different answers to the same question depending on who you ask. Still, spend time reading through the site, as there are some useful resources available. Better yet, go visit them (yes this is the third time we've mentioned this, for a reason). Sloan Admissions strongly encourages this, and you will learn a lot. You still won't know what to write in your essays, but you'll have a much better idea of what an MIT MBA is all about and why you might want to go there.

To whet your appetite for the cool stuff about MIT, we'll offer these key characteristics as a starting point for our discussion of how to attack your application:

- The MIT culture is truly collaborative – not just within the halls of the bschool, but all across campus. They even have a dual degree with the Harvard Kennedy School – they're happy to have you study at *another university* if you want. It's all about leveraging the best resources available.

  Another example of collaboration is that the entire MIT campus has a single entrepreneurship center – everyone accesses the same resources. Most other bschools have their own entrepreneurship center that's separate from any that the parent university might have. Not here. It's integrated. This is a clear benefit to Sloan students. This openness, and *true* collaboration, is unique. It's a school-wide community.

  Many bschools are islands unto themselves; they're often separated out from the main university, sometimes in an isolated part of the campus, or in other ways removed from the rest of the school. Not MIT. At MIT, you can expect to work on projects – or even form companies – not just with other members of your cluster, or incoming class, but with *undergrad students*. And those are some smart undergrads. These are kids inventing stuff. Maybe one of them has an idea for some new technology that you can leverage to build a company with?

- MIT is about entrepreneurship – but not just from a technology standpoint. Innovation has been a hallmark value at MIT for longer than at most bschools, mostly due to the engineering-heavy DNA of the underlying school, but also because they appreciate its value in a changing world – and in changing the world.

- MIT is smart. Yeah, you get firecrackers at every top school – but these MIT guys are scary smart. (Sorry but it's largely guys going to MIT – they are distant also-rans in the game of attracting women into their MBA program.) If you want to go to school with the sharpest knives in the shed, this is the place.

- MIT is about doing. It's about action. This is definitely a highly intellectual and academic place, but the overall culture, and certainly how admissions works, is about rewarding doers. They don't care about what you claim you want to maybe do some day; they want to arm you with the resources and watch you go do it.

MIT is strong in finance, entrepreneurship and innovation, and supply chain. They are one of the leaders in sustainability. They have the other stuff too – marketing and organizational behavior and all the standards. They train leaders. If you want to immerse yourself in a hands-on culture of achievers, people who've done stuff before and are working to do more, and greater, then this might be the perfect place for you.

What you should not expect at Sloan

We already mentioned that MIT has fewer female students on campus than some other top schools, coming it at only 34% of the 400 or so students. Yale and Cornell are in this same range. Not so impressive.

MIT is also not impressive in terms of diversity. There's no Consortium program at MIT. *They don't even list out the percentage of minorities in their class profile.* They have 55% U.S. citizens in their student population, which is actually lower than many other top MBA programs, so there's plenty of diversity at MIT – but their numbers of U.S. minorities are lower than at many other places.

Of course, some schools lump in Asian Americans with their "minority students" statistic, which is awfully misleading if you ask us. We feel that the "minority" stat should include only underrepresented groups like African Americans and Hispanics. Someone may technically be a minority in the overall population, but there's no shortage of Asians applying to bschool. For a school to include them in reporting their minority enrollment stats is a little lame. But we digress.

The point is that MIT will not lower their standards for you if you're a woman or a minority – and if you're in one of those demographic groups, you may feel like you're even more of a minority at MIT than you would elsewhere. Some other schools struggle with these issues too so it's not like there's something wrong with MIT, but we fail to see improvement in many of these metrics from year to year. We just aren't seeing this school put a big push towards making itself more diverse.

On one hand, this is a positive. MIT uses the same criteria for everyone. They don't need to compromise their standards in order to fill the class, as a larger program may be forced to do especially if it were chasing a goal of greater balance among race and gender. Even though MIT recently opened a brand-new building for the bschool, which we'd assume has greater capacity, they have no plans of increasing the MBA class size beyond the ~400 students that it is today. That's about 350 straight-up MBAs, and about 50 in LGO (Leaders of Global Organizations), a special dual-focus track managed in conjunction with MIT's engineering school (we'll offer insights on LGO in a bit).

Something else you should not expect at Sloan: A free ride. They don't offer full scholarships to anyone. They do have fellowships and grants – the LGO track in particular includes fellowship money – but it's never for the whole enchilada. We've heard of many candidates taking a pass on a Sloan admit only because another school was significantly more generous in what they were offering financially. The MIT MBA is not cheap, and going into it, you should expect to shoulder the bulk of the burden yourself.

What's Changed, and What's Stayed the Same

With the ongoing trend in bschools of *innovation* it seems that many schools are falling over themselves to reinvent the wheel. We can't count how many times a top school has announced that it's "the first" to implement some change in its curriculum or a new way of managing admissions – yet some other school has been doing things that way for awhile. This is definitely true with the scramble to integrate more real-world learning opportunities, both inside and outside the MBA classroom – yet MIT has had its Action Learning Labs in place for at least as long, if not longer, than any other top program.

MIT was also one of the first programs to launch a pre-experience Master's in Finance degree program for early-career candidates, and they've doubled its capacity since it first launched. Other aspects of MIT have remained remarkably consistent over a long period. As an example from the domain of admissions: They tend to interview the same number of applicants each year – 800, for a class size of around 400. That's typically around 20% of the applicant pool. Odds of getting in if you make it to the interview are quite good.

The big change in admissions is this new "essay" where you write your own recommendation. The schools have fewer essays these days in a bid to stay competitive; they know that if they have too many, that it will result in a decrease in apps. All the schools want to have a lot of apps. Even though they often say that an increase in applications doesn't coincide with an increase in quality of those apps, they still like to log higher numbers every year. This can affect their rankings, and it's a closely tracked metric within all school administrations. We heard that apps at MIT went down last year, even though that was the first year they cut their number of essays down to two. The main reason that we believe this happened is because their questions were just too difficult.

Unfortunately the worst of last year's two questions has been maintained this year too. Apparently they didn't feel that the submissions they received for that essay question were bad, but we can tell you that many many Brave Supplicants struggled mightily over what to write and how to write it. (We're talking about essay #1, "the mission"). Be prepared for some mental anguish as you figure out what they're asking for and how to present it.

The second essay last year was a behavioral question, which is the type of thing that MIT tends to ask in interviews. Those are questions like "Tell me about a time when..." They can be quite revealing for candidates and they're straightforward to develop – they still take a lot of work but there's no hidden trip-up elements lying in wait for you with them. We were dismayed to see that that behavioral question was the one to go, given that the "mission" question proved so difficult for people last year – and also considering how unwieldy and ridiculous this new "recommendation" question will be for people.

However, we can also appreciate why Sloan thought the recommendation would be a good thing. After all, for years (and years and years — something like thirty years in total) MIT asked applicants to the MBA program to write a cover letter seeking a spot in the MBA program. It was an exercise akin to applying for a job: You figure out why you're a match to the organization, and you try to articulate that succinctly to your reader.

This recommendation essay has traces of that, and we are certain that the MIT adcom was pleased with themselves on coming up with something new, that no other school is doing.

Of course, it's not entirely new — Kellogg had for many years as its own application staple an essay question where they said, "Imagine you are a student member of the admissions team. What would you say about your application to the Kellogg School?" That one was just as cumbersome and awkward to write as MIT's is bound to be. So unfortunately Sloan doesn't get brownie points for ingenuity with this.

The worst part of the new essay question? (Besides the fact that now they're telling you that you should write your own rec, whereas a theme that EssaySnark has had to beat over and over again for as long as we've been doing this is that you *can't* write your own rec — meaning, not the "real" ones that are submitted from other people on your behalf.)

The worst part is the the recommendation essay is asking for you to talk about the same type of stuff that would be viable for coverage in the mission essay.

Both of these essays are asking for proof of your past achievements and successes, so that the adcom can evaluate you in action.

The questions are asked in totally different ways, but both are best written from a professional perspective, covering examples that are drawn from your career. The approach and structure and content of each needs to be very different, but the underlying strategy needs to be identical: In both essays, you need to articulate how you have been a winner and a key contributor and a good teammate (or some other similar such stories), so that the adcom can see if you're going to be a good addition to their community.

You cannot repeat stories in both the essays. You need to explore new territory in each. But since both of them essentially have the same scope, then there's a real risk that you will be leaving some money on the table, in terms of how limited the view of yourself is that you'll be able to the adcom.

So what's stayed the same? Well, there is one advantage to how the admissions process is managed at this school, and that is that *only admissions peeps are doing the assessments*. At MIT, you won't have ANY student or alumni involved in the admissions process. Everyone reading your apps, doing your interviews, and making the final call on your candidacy are experienced admissions professionals — people who do this for a living. People who've been reading apps and interviewing candidates for years – and who've already gone through dozens or even hundreds of other applications before reading yours this year. Who know how the applicant pool is shaping up. Who are trained on the criteria MIT is looking for and how to evaluate it. Who can compare you against your peers in a way that is fair to all.

They've been doing it this way for years. This part, we sorta like it.

We also like that they do all their admissions work on iPads, and they started this years ago – definitely more embracing of technology than some other schools. So it's not like they're adverse to change. (Their use of iPads is why you cannot submit anything Flash-based as a multimedia presentation though – Steve Jobs and Adobe never did work that little disagreement out, did they?)

Having consistency in admissions is a good thing, and you'll get a fair shake with how your app is read. And the bottom line is that it doesn't actually matter to you if the essay questions are horrible or not. You'll do the best that you can with them – and you won't be at any disadvantage compared to anyone else, since everyone applying to Sloan has to deal with the same train wreck of an application. By going through this guide and understanding how to create a strategy within the constraints of these tough essay questions, you're giving yourself a big leg up over your competition who will struggle with the same questions and likely come up short.

If it was MIT's goal to make their job easier, by increasing the gap between the very-good essays and the mediocre to crappy ones, then indeed, this set of questions will surely serve that purpose.

So maybe MIT isn't so dumb about these things after all...

What MIT Is Looking For

Enough of our complaining about the essays. They are the reality that we need to deal with, so let's dig into what matters to you as a candidate to this program.

- **Leadership** – just like all the other schools – though how they assess this is unique

- **Maturity** – what's sometimes called "EQ", often evaluated through interpersonal relationship skills

- **Innovation** – not necessarily that you invented stuff, but that you can 'think outside the box'

- **Intellectual Horsepower** – demonstrated primarily through GMAT (or GRE) and GPA, with an emphasis on the quant side (they want you to participate in clubs etc. outside the classroom and you won't be able to do that if you're overwhelmed by the curriculum; a lower GMAT gives them pause because it means you may be working harder than necessary to stay afloat the first year)

- **Fit** – it should be obvious why you're applying to MIT, and even more so if your app is for LGO – just reading through your resume should give more than a hint as to why you're MIT material – your background should suggest that you're right for Sloan

The qualities that you need to convey for MIT's essays are also very important to present for Harvard – and other schools too, but especially for Harvard. Obviously, the way you tell your stories will need to change radically between HBS and Sloan, but similar topics may work for both, in terms of the core stories and examples that you'll be using to construct your MIT essays.

What all this boils down to is that *MIT puts the highest priority on actual experience.* They want to know what you have *already done* – not what you claim you may want to do some day, or some hypothetical intellectual exercise where you pontificate about the theories you have ...

Even despite the wording of MIT's first essay, they are not asking you to postulate about what you may do in the future. You need to be super careful with this one – we'll go into the details later on. It's not asking you for career goals. We can see how people might easily flub up on this one.

At MIT, they will be literally evaluating you based on what evidence you present of your past. They want to know what you've already done. If they see that you have a track record of success, they will be confident that you will continue that habit of high performance on into the future.

That, we're confident, is the genesis of the essay question about writing your own letter of recommendation. They want to see what's important about your background that says that you're ready for business school — and they want to see how you position those important bits.

We're going to be talking more about this, but the primary takeaway message at this early stage is:

Snarky Strategy #1

What works at MIT is
presenting a track record showing past success as a high achiever.

What doesn't matter? CAREER GOALS. Weird, huh? We'll explain why in a moment.

They care about what you have done in the past. They literally don't care about what you say you will do in the future.

In fact, they don't want to know about your future goals. If they did, they would ask you! They don't.

We can hear some people objecting already.

"But 'Snark! Isn't that what they're asking for in Essay 1?"

We say that it's not. Do you see the phrase "career goals" there? Or "professional objectives" or any other such thing? Sure, they are talking about "advancing the mission" - but if you're trying to claim that that's the same thing as your own career goals, then we're gonna argue with you. Please flip ahead to our discussion of Essay 1 starting on page 49 if you need more on this now.

This no-career-goals philosophy may be completely surprising to you, but it's true. That's not what they care about. Some people seem unable to write an MBA admissions essay without discussing their goals — it's like all the other schools have brainwashed them — so that's why we're giving you this caution upfront.

A Snarky Caveat

> Be very careful how you talk about your goals – or even *if* you talk about them. It would be fine if you avoided career goals in the MIT app entirely.

Perhaps this de-emphasis on career goals explains why about 85% of Sloan students are changing careers in some capacity or another. Maybe people who don't quite know what they want to do, just that they want to do something *different*, are attracted to Sloan.

So what exactly *are* they looking for, if they don't care about goals? How does MIT evaluate your past performance?

Minimums and Standard Qualifications

Just like any top school, a high GMAT and solid GPA are going to help you at MIT – but they're not the only factors that matter. Here's how the standard criteria of a profile are assessed at this school:

- **GMAT (or GRE – either is fine):** Your test score is not a measure of your competence – but it can be a measure of how seriously you take the idea of bschool. It is not easy to get a high score on one of these tests; to do so means that you put some work in. A **higher** GMAT is obviously better, and a decent quant score is important, but MIT does accept a range of scores.

    If you tested multiple times, submit your highest total score in the online application – however if your quant score was higher on the other test, then you may want to write the optional essay to call that to their attention. They'll see that in your history, so an essay about it isn't technically necessary, but you could make a specific point the other quant score as a way to present your case that you're qualified.

    What's a good-enough number for Sloan? Huge numbers of Sloan students have a 710 GMAT score, yet half as many come in with a 660 or 680 – it's totally possible to get into MIT with a score in that lower range. Average GRE math is reported at about 760 in the business school for those who opted for that test instead – mostly LGO students. The adcom told us recently that the full range of GMAT scores for the standard MBA program is 650 to 800, which means they're unwilling to go too low, but we do see plenty of people have success with scores below the 700 mark.

- **GPA.** Academics are taken seriously at Sloan, as another measure of your past performance. It's tough to get in if your GPA is too low (<3.0 on the 4.0 scale) – but it's not impossible. Because of the way they evaluate you, you are given opportunity to prove to them that you've got the chops to deal with the demanding curriculum that they serve up. Will a great GMAT score offset a low GPA? Sort of maybe not 100% but perhaps a little. If your poor GPA was a long time ago, then you have a better chance of a high GMAT helping you. If the college experience was very recent then it may be harder to convince them that you're serious about school, regardless of how high your GMAT score might be. The average GPA at Sloan is typically around 3.5 – slightly lower than HBS, Stanford, and Wharton, and on track with Columbia, Yale, and Kellogg. This is indicative of the smart kids who go there.

- **Reapplicants.** MIT accepts a large chunk of those who try again – they definitely appreciate it if you are that committed to them. Sometimes the only reason they reject someone is they feel the candidate needed a little more time in the workplace to build skills. They won't ever tell you this of course – that's why a reapplicant needs an objective review of what may have been your sins last year, before proceeding again (we can help with that if needed). In many cases, a reapplicant finds success at MIT simply through the process of better understanding how to express themselves in the app. You still need to show improvement – a higher GMAT score can make a difference for many – but you have a real shot as a repeat contender at this school.

- **International experience.** All top schools appreciate the value of time spent in foreign lands. This is probably not the most important thing to highlight in your MIT app for most people – they care about it, they just don't put a huge priority on it. It never hurts to be able to offer diversity of experiences in your profile. (We'll just mention here: MIT is specifically interested in increasing enrollment of European students – if you're from that part of the world, you may be welcomed especially warmly.)

- **Age and work experience.** Age is irrelevant; it's the nature and quality of the work and the contributions made that MIT cares about. LGO has a minimum of two years of work experience – three preferred – in order to apply, but there are no minimums for the MBA track. That doesn't mean they accept large numbers of youngsters. The average age at Sloan is older than some schools, with five or more years of work experience being quite common. We heard that for the Class of 2016, the average is 4.65, to be precise. But, the adcom comes at this with an open mind, and there's quite a few students (perhaps around 15%) who have just two years of experience.

If you are still in college, great! They'll be more than willing to look at your app for the regular MBA program – though EssaySnark has heard that it's very unusual to admit anyone who has literally no full-time work experience. Most likely, they would offer you a deferred admission, to let you go out and work a bit, before joining Sloan at a predetermined date in the future (usually after a year or two). This means that Sloan is a viable alternative to those who are gung-ho for the model of the HBS 2+2 program – MIT doesn't have it formalized with a separate track like HBS and Yale and Chicago do, but this option is available. As a younger candidate, you do have to convince them of your readiness for bschool. You'd need to demonstrate that you're operating ahead of your peers.

This is exactly what an older candidate has to do, too – or frankly, what ANY candidate has to do. The purpose of your essays is to show how you've approached the situations in your life, turned challenges into successes, and leveraged the opportunities around you – and the teams, and the organizations, and other resources – to create positive change for you and others. Whoever you are, they will want to learn about how you work on the inside, and how you translate that into action in the real world – and how you've got more to show for it in some respect or another than others in your peer group might.

How do they do that? How do they transform the stuff you present in your application into a form that allows them to do apples-to-apples comparisons with others?

Simple. They score you.

The MIT Competency Scale

They *score* you?

Yes, Brave Supplicant. They do.

While it may seem de-humanizing to break you down into little pieces and chunks as a way of evaluating your fit to the MBA program, this is in fact how the process essentially works at MIT. They have a bunch of things they're looking for – they call them "competencies." They have a scoring mechanism by which they rank you on each one. They tally it up and then compare candidates and figure out who to admit.

Let's remind you right here and now that you have a lot of influence over how this process turns out – after all, *who else is in control of the inputs?*

MIT Admissions isn't actually dissecting *you* – they're dissecting the way you've presented yourself. If you only offer superficial responses to the essay questions – or if you veer off on unrelated tangents that don't address the question they've asked at all – then that's what you're giving them to evaluate. And your app will then get weak scores. This isn't *you* getting weak scores; it's *your presentation.* They can only evaluate what you give them. So don't take it personally if you don't get in, and remember that your pitch needs to be rock-solid and comprehensive to have a shot.

Everything you present – the resume, the recommendations, and the essays, and then definitely the interview – will need to offer details about how you have navigated situations in your life and come up a winner. Not everything you've ever done needs to have a trophy associated with it – literally or figuratively – but even the challenging situations and problems you've faced need to give the adcom new information on how you operate.

Then, when the admissions person reads through your materials, they have something to go on. They have something substantial to examine for evidence that you have certain traits. They will be ranking your app on these particular dimensions, and then they'll add up the scorecard to have a total for you.

No, EssaySnark is not on the Sloan admissions team. No, we don't have insider information on what the actual dimensions are, or what the scale is. But we've done a lot of research into this, and MIT themselves is pretty candid about it. They explicitly say that it's 8 dimensions, for example. And we're pretty sure that it's a 5-point scale, 1 being lacking or minimal, 5 being superlative, for each dimension. You're not expected to have a 5 on each; they know you're stronger in some areas than others. They seek a balance across the class, and they want to see an assortment of qualities in you, too.

EssaySnark's research has resulted in a list of 7 competencies that we'd be willing to bet are among the 8 used by the Sloan admissions team. We can't guarantee that we nailed those 7, and obviously we're missing one entirely – but we'd stake real money on at least four of them being spot-on accurate. These relate to the traits you'd expect: leadership, innovation, etc. (no, those aren't the competencies – the competencies are actually behavioral markers, or indicators, that *point to* umbrella labels like "leadership").

So we did all this research, thinking that we'd flat-out tell you what these competencies are in this *Guide*... And then we realized that it would be professionally inappropriate to do so.

So no, we won't be sharing our list.

Why not? Because it won't be doing anyone any favors.

1. If MIT Sloan wanted the competencies known, they would publish them. It doesn't seem right for us to do so ourselves. (Plus, what if we're wrong??)

2. If you know – or *think you know* – what the competencies are, you're going to try and write your essays around them. This would not serve you, no, not at all. In fact, it could cause you to shoot yourself in the foot.

Several of the competencies are expressed in language that only an academic – or a shrink – could understand. They're all fancy-sounding. They're a little hard to tease apart, frankly. What if we listed them out, but nobody understood what they meant? Talk about doing you a disservice!

Even if you 100% understood what they were, writing your essays around the competencies would lead you straight into that trap of trying to say what you think they want to hear – which is what MIT, of all places, objects to the strongest.

The other problem is that there's *8* of them (well, we've only figured out what 7 of them might be – but still). You would have a complete #essayfail if you tried to focus on seven different attributes in writing out your drafts. Your head would split in pieces and your brain would roll out onto the floor.

Plus, MIT would be *pissed* at us. We don't want any of the schools to resent our very existence. We much prefer being friends with those folks.

We wouldn't be doing anyone any favors by publishing this information, us, you, or them.

And remember, nobody is expected to have all eight competencies. You don't need to know them. You just need to present who you are in an effective way, and we're convinced that those competencies will naturally be revealed.

So here's what we're going to do – since we recognize that some of you will feel that you *need to know what these are!!!*

First, please be assured that regardless of how they may have constructed this list of 8 competencies, the actual traits MIT is looking for are not mysterious or exotic. They're what all top schools look for. You don't have to know any secret code to unlock the MIT treasure. Just read their website. They are quite forthcoming with what they want.

Next, you should also know that EssaySnark examines application materials from Brave Supplicants we work with through the lens of the respective school's adcom – at least, as much as an outsider possibly can. We practically stalk these schools to understand what they're looking for in a candidate, and we have years of data collected on outcomes of previous Brave Supplicants, to help us analyze your profile against those who have gone before. We will be using our understanding of MIT's competency scale in reviewing any essays that you submit to us for a paid critique.

If you are obsessing over these competencies, then submit your essays for the Essay Decimator service, and when we review your *revised drafts* (not your first drafts) in the second stage of that process – if you ask us for it, then when we return your drafts, we will also share with you our list of the 7 competencies that we've ferreted out. We won't send them out unless you request them.

We hope you understand our position on this. We've simply seen it backfire too many times – an earnest Brave Supplicant struggles with what to say in his essays, and thrashes about, thinking that the goal is to *impress the reader*, and he gets distracted. He ends up trying to *solve the problem of writing an essay* rather than simply *answering the question in a direct and honest manner*.

This happens A LOT with you engineer types – and since there's A LOT of those types interested in MIT, then we feel it's our duty to try and save you from yourself.

Here's all you need to know to be successful with your Sloan app

You don't need no stinkin' competencies.

What you need is to come up with your own authentic, detailed, and honest answers to the essay questions.

You need to wrestle with those questions and spend a lot of time reflecting on the situations that you have been in that may be relevant to each one, and figure out what you can tell the adcom about how you handled yourself – and you need to trust the process.

If you write a thorough response to each question that conforms to the instructions that they've laid out for you – with a sincere answer that's targeted to just what they've asked – you will be fulfilling your duties. You will be giving the adcom what they need in order to assess you along this spectrum of traits they're interested in.

You don't have to worry about the psychological gobbledygook that some smart people came up with in devising this list of competencies. In fact, we hope you'll put it out of your mind, as we honestly believe it can get in your way as you go through this process.

Instead, focus on the questions. Don't write to the competencies; write from what's real.

MIT is not looking for a specific background. They don't have a "type." They're looking for excellence in whatever you have done. They want to see where you have made an impact. They will be comparing you to your peer group and looking for these traits that they know lead to success in their program.

These tend to be:

- Performing better than your peer group – in your career, on the GMAT, in college – in life.
- Leadership, which can be defined in many ways, such as: convincing someone to do something; taking the initiative; getting buy-in; etc. etc. etc.
- Teamwork; how you interact with others; are you down to earth?

When you write your drafts, you can step back and look at them through that lens. Ask yourself, how is this essay demonstrating a strength of mine?

Don't worry, we'll offer more guidance on how to do this in the pages that follow.

First, let's get down and dirty with the Leaders for Global Organizations program that MIT offers.

What's LGO and Should You Apply to It?

We already mentioned a few factoids along the way about LGO – Leaders for Global Organizations. It used to be called *LFM – Leaders for Manufacturing* – and we sorta think that was more descriptive, given what this program is. This special joint-degree program has been around for quite awhile, since the late '80s. It has a great reputation among industry and placement rates tend to be high.

Despite the "global" in this name, this is primarily for those interested in an intensive supply chain, logistics, or ops focus to their MBA studies. This unique program is a joint offering with the MIT School of Engineering. The only comparable option in any other top bschool is Kellogg's MMM track with Northwestern's McCormick School.

If you are going into product manufacturing – specifically with the intention to focus on outsourcing in Asia (that's where the "global" comes from apparently) – then MIT LGO is the place for you. Basically you need to want to *build stuff* in order for this to be the right program for you. Our impressions are that if you want to go into consulting for these companies, this might be overkill. You should do your own research to find out if it's the right fit for you.

MIT has a dedicated website for LGO so we're not going to go into too much here; the requirements are spelled out clearly by MIT themselves. A few points to offer:

- It's totally fine to apply to LGO if you already have a master's in engineering; that's actually a common educational profile of their students.

- Only about 50 students are admitted to LGO each year – but they don't get huge volumes of applications to this program either, so the admit rates tend to be almost reasonable, as those things go: They average around 300 applications per year, and they always interview around 100 candidates, so your chances are actually quite good.

- The average GMAT for LGO students in the Class of 2016 is 712, which is down from the 720 that they have for the current second-years (Class of 2015). These figures are remarkable given that the LGO cohort is so darned small. This means that anyone who wants to have a real shot at LGO is going to need to have a very good GMAT score. They also accept the GRE for this so it's fine to move ahead with your app if that's the score you have on hand.

Perhaps the most important tidbit to know about LGO is this: Because of the increased courseload required for the joint degree, there's more work obviously – and less opportunity for networking. You'll start in June instead of August, to get a head start on the engineering coursework before the MBA cohort lands at campus later in the summer. The LGO students tend to bond quite closely, however there's just 50 of them, compared to 350 in the larger MBA class. You're probably not going to get to know that larger student body as well as you would if you were only an MBA student. And you might have not much free time overall.

We've heard that this is what it's like for the MMM students over at Kellogg, too (and Lauder students at Wharton, for what it's worth). You're taking on more with these joint programs. The internships are engineering-based, rather than management-based, so you can expect a bit more of a constrained path on what's expected. You won't be in the same free-for-all of on-campus recruiting for your summer internship that the MBA cohort goes through. The LGO internships are more hand-selected based on corporate partners to the program. There's also a thesis that you'll need to write at the end, like most other Master's programs (outside of the MBA) require. More work. Be prepared for it. You'll come out of it with a great specialization, but there are always tradeoffs to be aware of.

There is only one single deadline for LGO, which comes in December. If you're not accepted to MIT LGO, then you'll be automatically considered with the other Round 2 applicants to the standard Sloan MBA program.

The rest of this *Guide* is focused on the standard MBA program, though an LGO applicant will likely find value here too. In past years, LGO has had many more essays than MBA, and the application requirements are quite different, which we assume will be the same again this year (their website has not been updated as of the time of this writing). Study those carefully before proceeding – some of what follows will not apply in your case, and you need to get a handle on what's expected so you don't flub it up.

Important Nuances and Differences with an MIT Application

There's a couple differences in policies at MIT that are worth noting:

- **TOEFL.** Refreshingly, MIT does not require the TOEFL. Not for anyone. They use your essays, and especially your interview, to determine your English skills. Yale has dropped the TOEFL too and we can only guess that it's because MIT has had the policy for years. If you're an international student interested in MIT, then great - one less thing to worry about!

- **Test expirations.** For this year's application (Class of 2017), the GMAT or GRE score you report must be from a test taken no later than September 1, 2010. Many schools have loosened their test acceptance timeframes so that scores need only be valid (less than five years old) at time of application, not at time of matriculation. MIT has not made this change. Doublecheck the date on any older test you want to use, to make sure it will be valid for your MIT application.

- **Recommendations.** MIT requires the standard two recs; both must be from people in a supervisory position to you. No peer recs, and never submit a rec from a family member. If you've been at the same job for three years, they'd prefer both recs from that workplace (just make sure they cover different aspects of your candidacy). Make sure your recs are submitted when the deadline comes. MIT will hold your app for a day or so past the deadline to wait for a missing rec, but if it doesn't arrive, they will review your application WITHOUT THAT RECOMMENDATION. That's not to your benefit. Recs add a lot of value, you want them included in the evaluation. Other schools will bump the app to the next round if it's missing recs on deadline day. Not sure which is better. Mostly this means, follow up with those recommenders and make sure they come through for you on time! Also, with past year's MIT apps, technically applicants could submit three recommendations, but we do NOT advise this. The adcom reviewer has a choice of selecting only two, since that's all that are required – and there's no guarantee they will choose the best two. Figure out which of your recommenders will do the best job on your behalf, and go with them.

- **Pre-reqs.** Introductory calculus and microeconomics must be taken before starting your MBA. If you don't have those on your transcripts you can either take them now or wait till you're admitted and then do them in the summer before you begin at Sloan. Taking a free MOOC through Coursera or Khan Academy is not going to satisfy this requirement, though it may be worth mentioning something like that somewhere in the application (Optional Information) as a way to shore up a weakness in your quant profile. For the formal pre-reqs, you'll want to go to an accredited university and have an official transcript to present when you're done. Lacking these classes at time of app review won't negatively affect your chances so don't worry about taking them early unless you're simply inspired to do so – or, if you have some weakness in the quant area of your profile that you want to offset.

- **Deferrals.** This is one of the only top schools that might consider a request for deferring your start date to the following year. Most schools pre-empt all such requests by saying that deferrals are never granted. MIT will consider a request – but you'd better have a good reason. The most common case where a deferral is granted is for a college student who wants to go work for a year or so. Lots of people ask for deferrals as a way to play their cards at another school – maybe they're on the waitlist at a different bschool and hope for that to pan out, so they don't want to commit to Sloan just yet. Typically you'd need to pay a hefty non-refundable deposit in order for this to work. Our advice? If you want to ask for a deferral – pay that deposit FIRST, and then hit the admissions office up with your request. You'll be in a stronger position and they'll be more likely to grant it. Deferrals are quite rare so just because they're open to them doesn't mean they're easy to get.

These are part of an assortment of unique policies in effect in the Sloan admissions. The big difference at MIT is the **overall admissions cycle itself.**

The rule of thumb for most schools is "apply either in Round 1 or Round 2." Since MIT just has two rounds, does that mean you're fine if you apply in either one?

NO.

When to apply

Apply to MIT in Round 1 if at all possible.

Wait – this is more important than that.

Snarky Strategy #2

> Do everything in your power
> to apply to MIT in Round 1.

If the Round 1 deadline has already passed, all is not lost. Round 2 is still very doable for a strong candidate.

But Round 1 is *way more doable*.

Why?

1. This is the only school that admits *half the class in each round*.
2. And, they get significantly fewer apps in the first round.

Do the math. Your chances are better in Round 1.

This is particularly true if you're coming from an oversubscribed candidate pool – basically, anyone of an Asian origin. Or an engineer. Engineers aren't the "oversubscribed candidate pool" automatically but MIT does get a lot of them.

If that's you, PLEASE pull out all the stops and get your app in for the first round.

The big disadvantage with the MIT process is that you'll get your Round 1 decision quite late – in fact, some other Round 1 schools may be asking for you to pay a deposit by then if they've accepted you. MIT has moved its Round 1 deadline up this year so we're hoping that means they'll also move up their decision dates – in past years, you wouldn't get a final word from MIT until late in January. It's even worse if you applied to the LGO class, where our understanding is that decisions are announced in early March (or at the end of February depending on whether you believe the LGO website or the MBA website).

Because of these realities, sometimes people end up paying a deposit at their second-choice school to secure a spot, then forfeit that when MIT comes back with a 'yes.' It's an expensive way to go but it might be worth it as an insurance policy.

The biggest issue with this is *you probably won't know your MIT Round 1 decision until after Round 2 deadlines for most schools.* This one is in the category of supreme suckyness. It's possible that MIT is changing its processes this year to better accommodate the overall admissions cycle, but they haven't breathed a word of it yet so we are doubtful.

Here's how the sequence often goes down:

You most likely would get an interview invitation at MIT in the November / December timeframe for a Round 1 app – or, you might have had your application "released" by them in advance of that, if they know that they're not interested in you. So you should have at least an indication of how things might be going with your Sloan chances by the time you would need to decide on whether Round 2 applications are necessary. You will need to have other schools' Round 2 apps well underway by end of November, just as a point of reference – you need that much time to write essays. But you won't have a definite yes/no answer from them.

So what this means is that you probably will need to plan on some Round 2 apps, if you're applying to MIT as a first-choice school in Round 1. It makes for a more extended application cycle for Sloan wanna-bes than for most other candidates. This is a downside to some of the good parts of this admissions cycle.

Why don't they have a Round 3?

For as long as we've been doing admissions consulting (which is a long time – we're not going to say exactly how long), MIT has only had the two rounds, with deadlines falling in a similar spot on the calendar each year. In this regard, they have resisted the "peer pressure" coming from the other schools (actually, coming from the hordes of impatient Brave Supplicants clamoring to know their decisions) to tighten their cycle times and move their schedules up.

We have never asked them, but our assumption is that they don't have a Round 3 because they don't need one. They can fill their class with just two. They know that enough motivated candidates will be applying in the first two rounds, and they gear their processes around that. This is true at all the schools; very few candidates get admitted in the last round at any of them. But other schools hang onto that third round – and probably will continue to do so as long as Harvard does. Once Harvard changes, others will surely follow. MIT doesn't have the same clout so in this regard so them having just two rounds makes them an outlier instead of a trend-setter.

What not to do

We'll get to the essays in a minute. First let's mention a short list of things to avoid in your MIT application.

- **Do not speak in generalities.** Don't talk about how you excelled on the project and impressed your boss, and thus got a promotion. Instead, tell the reader what you *did*. Words like "excelling" and "promotions" are not that helpful for you; they're just the start in sharing your story. It's very, very important to be specific in describing how you brought change to the organization or what you literally did to get something done. The MIT adcom tells you this much directly, in more than one place. The essay questions come with instructions saying you should talk about what you *thought, felt, said, and did.* Take these instructions quite literally. The reader needs to see evidence of your skills and abilities through the stories you choose, and through how you tell them. This is true for all schools, but perhaps none more so than Sloan, for all the reasons we already laid out.

- **Do not skip the Optional Question.** This is *not* the same as every other school's "optional essay" - instead, at Sloan, the Optional Question is just like NYU Stern's Personal Expression essay: It's optional, but it's mostly an *opportunity* for you, and in this case you should go for it. But for Sloan (and for NYU too, ideally) try to skip the writing. Don't do another essay. Instead, do something really revealing – like a video. Or anything conveyed in any type of multimedia format (audio or video – YouTube is especially inviting in this regard – PowerPoint also might work). We'll talk more about this later. You won't want this to be the basic stuff that other schools' optional essays might be. You want to use this with a strategy. Don't skip your chance to share the "real you" with the adcom in this way.

- **Do not worry about applying early.** While it's always wise to get your application in before the day of the deadline, to avoid the traffic jam on the school's servers and any technical glitches (and stress) that may arise, there is no benefit to submitting a MIT application early. Some schools encourage you to submit early. MIT doesn't. You get no special brownie points for submitting a month early versus on the last day.

  That being said, you do not want to procrastinate with your MIT app, since crafting strong essays will take many rounds of revision, and you need to give yourself time for that in-depth process. Plan on spending at least a month doing rewrites (yes, as in 30 days).

- The biggest "don't do this" at MIT Sloan? **Don't write about career goals.**

MIT MBA and Goals (or lack thereof)

We laid this out in the beginning of this *Guide* yet we think it deserves a larger discussion.

If you've read through the *SnarkStrategies Guide* on Columbia or other schools, you may be wondering about the difference in emphasis between these schools. In a Columbia, or Duke, or Haas, or NYU application, the career goals are the most important angle. In fact, for many many other schools, the goals are primary. Well-articulated goals are considered paramount. Even HBS asks about them in the online application.

Not so at MIT. **They don't ask about career goals anywhere** – not in your essays, not in your interviews, not any questions for the recommenders. Nowhere. They honestly *do not care.*

Well maybe they care – but they don't use it evaluate you. MIT Sloan does not solicit anything about career goals as part of your MBA application because they know that:

1. You have no idea what you want to be when you grow up
2. Your goals will change radically when you go through the process of earning your MBA
3. If they did ask about goals, you will simply tell them what you think they want to hear – you'll make stuff up to answer the question

All adcoms are aware of these truths, however different admissions teams have different philosophies (obviously!) in how they manage the process of filling their entering class. MIT is not interested in having you shine them on; they don't want to go through the motions of hearing you be all earnest and sincere about this thing that you really are clueless about.

Now, EssaySnark quite frankly thinks that you need to have at least some sort of a clue about what you want to do with your life *before* you start your MBA education, else you'll not be able to take advantage of the opportunities that bschool presents.

For one thing, do you know what other careers pay? Are you aware of what you may be qualified for, in terms of a future job, coming out of school? If you have a family to support especially, it seems like these are very valid questions to be hammering through NOW, before you apply.

From our perspective, there is value in going through these thought processes early on, to determine at least some ideas of what you may want to pursue in the future. And how in heck do you know you need an MBA if you don't even know what you want to do with it? So there's a purpose to asking about goals.

You also should be identifying MBA programs, at least in part, based on what they specialize and their success in placing graduates into the field that you're interested in. (In case you're curious, MIT sends a huge number of graduates to consulting – and perhaps surprisingly, they send more people to strategy consulting than they do to tech consulting. Investment banking and other finance jobs are also quite common to break into through Sloan's connections.) If you don't know what you want to specialize in then how can you pick the right school?

But the MIT adcom doesn't like this approach of looking at the school's placement data to see if they're a good fit for you as a candidate. Sloan feels that it's misguided to choose a school based on career goals. We see their point – but only to an extent.

Blasphemous or not, we just don't buy the position that bschool is exclusively about the education. That's too much a purist's perspective for our taste. Yeah yeah yeah you're going back to school to *learn stuff* – we do hate it when BSers forget that part. But the MBA is a much more practical degree than most other graduate programs. And it's frickin' expensive. You need to be realistic and look at what you will ACTUALLY gain from the experience. And sometimes that comes down to hard-and-fast assessments of dollars and cents. And typically *that* means, looking at career opportunities.

In terms of your application to Sloan, you will not need to talk about this at all.

Oh wait {screech on the brakes} there is one important program at MIT where goals play a part in admissions.

If you're applying to the early-career track Master in Finance at MIT, then you do need to talk about goals. Most people reading this Guide are not targeting that program, but just in case you are, you need to be very aware that goals should be discussed in that essay. They include it in the application instructions ("Describe your short and long-term professional goals. How will our MFin degree help you achieve these goals?") and you should not overlook that angle when you write your essay.

But for a regular ol' MBA application to MIT Sloan – for full-time or for LGO – you may want to explicitly AVOID mentioning anything related to your career. If you already know what you want to do and why you want to go to MIT to do it, fine, mention it within Essay 1, or maybe include it in the "recommendation" that you're going to write for yourself. Just make sure that you can back it up with some evidence. This needs to come through as a PASSION for you, something legit that you're committed to and already working towards – not just some noble idea that you think makes you look.

You will not be penalized for not breathing a mention anywhere in your Sloan application about what you want to do with your future career.

You *might* be penalized if you come across sounding like a me-too candidate who tosses out some impressive-sounding goal but doesn't have any authentic reasons to back it up.

If you focus on career goals too much in your MIT apps, they will simply assume that you have not done your research on what they're about, and they will know that you're applying to other schools that are obsessed about goals. This would not be in your favor.

Before you freak out on that last part: All the schools know that everyone is applying to multiple schools. They don't mind that. What they do mind is if you are not showing them why THEY are your first choice. It's just like dating: you gotta love the one you're with.

Actually, that multiple-apps thing is a good thing to share with you. Let's discuss how to manage the project of applying to MIT in conjunction with the other apps you'll be tackling.

MIT and Your Multi-School Strategy

The work you put in to laying the foundation of your MIT essays will possibly be re-usable to an extent for some other schools. The essays themselves will not.

It may work less well the opposite direction – meaning, the ideas you come up with for presentation in other schools' essays might not translate too much to a good MIT strategy.

And, even though there are only two true essays does not mean that your MIT application will be the easiest one to knock out. You'll need to do a significant amount of brainstorming, and reflection, and hammering out and reworking your message, in order to develop the material that communicates "you" in the way you need it to for these questions.

The work you do to figure out how to present yourself to MIT will likely be useful for other schools, whether in their essays or when you go to interview, just based on the amount of effort that the MIT essay questions will force upon you. But you cannot expect that an essay you've written for a different school will easily work for one of the MIT questions, nor vice versa. Which leads us to:

Which order should you do your apps in?

This depends on what other schools you're applying to.

Snarky Strategy #3

> You do not want to do your MIT essays first, because they're hard. But you also need to do them early, so that you can get your recommenders moving on their own tasks.

The first essays you do will be a challenge; it's a learning process, and you don't want to have to deal with figuring out this essay-writing business on the hardest schools in the universe. You also don't want to do MIT last, because you'll be burned out, and you won't be as likely to muster up the energy to do a good job on such a difficult set of writing.

Ideally, you will cut your teeth on essays that are more straightforward – such as for Berkeley-Haas, who has what we call the Goldilocks essays this year. Or Tuck. Or even Columbia. Then do MIT as your second. You can't put MIT off too long, because you have to get that strategy down solid before you can go to your recommenders (see below on that).

One note on Columbia, since we mentioned them: If you like Columbia more than MIT, then definitely do the Columbia Early Decision option along with MIT Round 1. If Columbia says yes, you'll hear pretty early in the cycle (relatively speaking) and you can withdraw your MIT app from consideration.

However, if you only *think* you like Columbia more – but you haven't based this opinion on any hard data like *visiting the schools* – then we encourage you to get yourself on campus in Boston first. We have seen more than one BSer apply to Columbia in the Early Decision process, and only after that app was in did they go to visit MIT – and then they regretted their hastiness in choosing Columbia. Don't pull the trigger on a Columbia ED app unless you're certain they are your first choice school.

Back to MIT.

Which order should you tackle the MIT components in?

Since we're talking about which order you should do what, here's another important tip to consider:

Snarky Strategy #4

> Write your essays first – and get your strategy down solid. Then hit up your recommenders to do their thing.

The new MIT essay question where you write your own recommendation puts a very unfortunate complication into the entirety of your application planning process. Why? Because you need to know what YOU plan to say in your own recommendation, before you can have a rational conversation with your recommenders about what THEY should be saying.

If *your* recommendation ends up covering the exact-same stuff that *your recommenders'* recommendations do, well, that's a real missed opportunity.

At the same time, there should be at least *some* overlap. If you're finding something important enough to present in your own recommendation letter, then surely your recommenders would feel the same. To have no shared examples between the three application assets would look really quite strange.

Yes, this is complicated.

It also means that you probably need to do your MIT essays first, before you do any other schools' – because you want to have your queue-up conversations with your recommenders only once, laying out their task and deliverables in a single meeting so that they can get to work on all your applications together. It would truly suck for you to have to go back to your recommenders and ask them to adjust their focus in this one one-off application for MIT. That would especially suck if they'd already started working on the recommendations and your request would mean more work for them.

You can have your recommenders add value in a very targeted way if you approach them correctly. And usually, that means approaching them *after* you know what your platform or theme is – which is important for all schools, but which is critically important with this crazy MIT application this year. So you can't expect to have that conversation with your recommenders until after you've developed out the essays to at least draft 2. And preferably till they're close to done (draft 3 or later).

What EssaySnark suggests is, **get through at least the first couple drafts of your MIT essays before talking to your boss about writing any recommendations.** Then you'll know what you'll be talking about in your own "recommendation" and you can figure out which examples will be good ones for your recommender to underscore by presenting again – and, you'll know where the holes are in your profile, and you can suggest ideas for what your boss can talk about that can fill those holes.

If you want more advice on this and other critical strategies, check out the Letters of Recommendation App Accelerator (see essaysnark.com for details).

Snarky Strategy #5

Do your resume last.

This is also counter-intuitive for many people. It seems like you'd want to knock the low-hanging fruit of the resume off early and be done with it.

Oh wait. You didn't realize you needed to re-do your resume?

You do. It's almost a guarantee that you will need to, at a minimum, reword the bullets on your resume. You might also need to update it if it's not current. And many people have much more extensive work to do on formatting and layout – and stripping out unnecessary content. (You don't need that line about computer skills, for example. Everyone knows Excel at this point – and if you don't know it, you should if you're applying to bschool! Take that off, it's wasted space.)

You should not do the resume overhaul until after you know your theme. You need to have your platform established – and you need to have a good idea of what you'll be covering in your essays – before you will be sufficiently equipped to do a bang-up job of revising the resume. So push that off to a little later if you can.

As with everything app-related, EssaySnark offers additional support and resources on the resume on our website at essaysnark.com.

OK. We know what you're thinking. "EssaySnark, when are we going to get to the essays?"

How about now?

Brainstorming and Prep Work for the Sloan Application

You need to mine your raw material before you start to answer any of these essay questions. You have to know what you *might* say before you begin to decide where you would say it. There could be some slicing and dicing among the different essay questions as you first design your strategy. In order for that to be effective then you need to know what material is available to work with.

We recommend doing some brainstorming around why you want to go to MIT, and around your biggest and best accomplishments and contributions. If you're stuck, we have an app for that — the Accomplishments & Achievements App Accelerator is designed specifically for essay questions like these. Before trying to start writing any essays, you should comb through your raw material and start to examine which stories will be best to present to the adcoms.

Don't focus specifically on the Sloan questions during this process. Instead, just figure out the things you've done in your life that are notable and which could be worth mentioning. What would you want to talk about in a job interview, for example?

These should already be on the resume — but don't expect to find your best material already pre-defined there. We rarely encounter a resume that's already optimized with this stuff. You might want to not even look at your resume at the beginning of your list-creation process, so that your thinking doesn't become limited by the entries you've already got down there. You can dig out the resume later in your brainstorming, to make sure you haven't omitted anything — but if you start off with the resume, it may prevent you from remembering all the good stuff organically.

Before you focus on your past, do some work reflecting on the "mission" part of the question — this is one of the (many) tricky parts of the Sloan application and you're going to need to do extensive thinking and reflecting on it in order to nail it.

Why do you want to go to MIT?

This is not explicitly asked for in either of the Sloan essays, but it is implicit in what they're looking for in Essay 1. You can't just ponder this question for five minutes and write an answer; you'll need to mentally chew on this one. It's a non-trivial question, particularly how it's laden down with the "mission" angle that they've asked. Set yourself some time to really look at these different components and angles.

Let's start off by the simple bit: What has attracted you to MIT? Why do you want to go there for your MBA?

If you want to offer a directional target about your career interests in answer to this question, fine – but not necessary nor recommended. Some people seem compelled to include that, and we can't fault you for it. We'd much rather see concrete reasons for wanting the MBA and wanting to go to Sloan to get it that do not dwell on on future goals There should be plenty of reasons you can cite for Sloan (or any school) about your rationale for choosing them.

Here's some room to explore this.

Why do you need an MBA? (Try to answer this without stating your career goals.)

Why do you specifically need (or want) to go to MIT Sloan?

This is where you will go beyond what you've read on the website (though that information could be relevant). This is where you leverage what you know about MIT, from all the research you've done — you have visited the school, right? This is how they see that you understand what they are about.

Where not going to tell you why you want to go to MIT. That would be a little ridiculous, wouldn't it? Reasons for choosing a school and why you want an MB A in the first place are personal. These answers are up to you and you alone. The adcom just wants you to be genuine and honest.

The core of your pitch for MIT needs to center around your accomplishments, so let's start to look at those.

How many accomplishments?

You need to have a bunch. They're asking for "examples" (plural – at least two) in Essay 1, and in Essay 2 you will ideally tell a few new stories – probably even more fully fleshed out than the ones in the first essay – about additional specific accomplishments. And, your recommenders need to talk about some cool stuff you've done, too, preferably some of that being new cool stuff that you aren't already covering in your essays. So how many accomplishments? A lot.

Initially you should simply begin the ideation process by figuring out everything and anything that might possibly qualify as a good accomplishment example. Your final product of your essays probably will have four accomplishments total, maybe five, but don't limit yourself to identifying any certain numbers at the beginning.

Why don't you jot down here the ones you're thinking about right now. If you come up with lots of choices, it'll be easier down the road when you have to figure out which are best for the essays.

While the Sloan essays ask you to focus on things from the past three years, for the purpose of this exercise you don't have to limit yourself — try to simply get the juices flowing in how you think about all the great and cool things that you have done. You also need not limit yourself to only professional examples. Come up with instances of success from any aspect of your life, unfettered. Unlock your brain and let some ideas tumble out.

My most significant accomplishments are:

_____

_____

_____

_____

_____

_____

_____

OK, that's a good start — and maybe you already defined those in your work on another school's application. Accomplishments are a good way to demonstrate leadership and they're appropriate to present in lots of essays.

Let's tease apart the Sloan prompt in this context now — ask yourself this series of questions — we recommend going through this list and FORCING yourself to answer each one individually. Set aside at least 20 minutes to work on these. Do not just breeze through this section and neglect to try and answer these. Wrestle them down. Make yourself spit out SOEMTHING in response to each one.

Here you go — these should keep you busy for awhile:

Two or three times that I was innovative were:

_____

_____

_____

_____

_____

Innovation can mean lots of things – it doesn't just mean creating a new product or inventing something. Innovation can be a way of thinking about a problem, or doing something in a way it hadn't been done before. This needs to be more than just ideas – you need to have examples where you followed through and implemented it, not just that you had a brilliant inspiration come into your mind. Innovation can be about problem-solving, it can be about an "aha!" moment, it can be about putting the same pieces together in a new way. Don't limit yourself just to work stories during this brainstorming, it's fine if you come up with ideas from other parts of your life – sometimes, thinking about good examples from one context will help trigger the ideas from another.

The "innovative" angle comes into play in two parts of the prompt for Essay 1 – they're talking about "innovative leaders" and they've also got the part about "generating ideas that advance management practice." You should explore both these sides as you do your brainstorming on "innovation."

In fact, you might even want to do some brainstorming on the *definition* of innovation – you could make a list that goes something like "An example of innovation would be..." and then fill in the blank with a series of hypotheticals. Sometimes if you list out what you've observed in others, it helps you remember a time when you expressed it yourself.

Two or three times that I acted on my principles were:

_____

_____

_____

_____

This can be times when your ethics were challenged, or that you had to do the right thing. It can be a time when you stood up for yourself or for someone else. It can be a time when someone else was lying and you told the truth. It's best to find examples where you ACTED – not when you *didn't act* – as a way to demonstrate principles. In other words, don't talk about a time when you *could have stolen something because no one was looking, but you didn't* – that's not good, all it does is shows that you were tempted to steal! You don't get brownie points for obeying the law.

Instead, find examples where your actions put you out on a limb with someone or you had to take a personal risk to assert your principles in some way. Those are more powerful.

Where have I advanced a mission?

_____

_____

_____

_____

This language sounds a little grandiose or militaristic but that doesn't mean your examples must be all high-minded and lofty. See if you can think of a time or two when you had an objective or goal to meet – some big project you were working on, or an idea you wanted to implement – or even better, an initiative with a shared deliverable. A group or team thing, for your company or the client. When you are just doing your job, then you're a cog in the machine letting everything hum along – but when you do something that *advances the mission*, then that's when your actions made a big difference. See if you can think of a time when the contribution you made moved the project to the next level, or how your work accelerated progress for others – where you worked at a level beyond your peers. Those examples can be excellent stories to share with the adcom.

What team environments have I been a part of?

_____

_____

_____

_____

There aren't any explicit questions about "teams" in the two MIT essay questions, but teamwork is always valued by these top schools, and that angle is implicit in their set of questions on the recommendation essay, when they ask about how you "interact with other people." There are plenty of alternate ways that that question can be addressed however it would be great if you had one marquee story across all the essays that covered you as a top performer in a team-based context. This one may end up working better from your recommenders' recommendations (instead of the one you write for yourself) but it would be best if you at least had one solid story to use somewhere – or more, if you can think of them.

When have I influenced others?

_____

_____

_____

_____

To extend your thinking around the question in the recommendations for "how you interact with other people", try to think of a time when you had to advocate for your ideas, and you steered other people in the direction you wanted to go. This type of example is the most vivid when you had a bold new idea, or you were proposing something that was initially quite unpopular; it's easier to see the impact in such stories, and it would give you an opportunity to focus in on some of your soft skills in action. This can have real value in the application. Again, this example is one that might work better for your recommender to talk about – or not. Or, both. Remember, you could potentially be covering a story in your own "recommendation" that your recommender also chooses to talk about.

Switching gears slightly for this next one:

Where have I pushed myself outside my comfort zone?

This is actually the question that they asked for Essay 2 last year — and it's a good one to reflect upon as you work through your raw material. If you're interested in anything entrepreneurial in your future, then stories about taking a risk, doing the unexpected, going beyond the status quo can play quite well (yes we know that we said not to talk about your goals, but sometimes they seep through into the essays anyway, and so that's why we mention this tip here). Look for an example where you took a risk — an intelligent risk, but one that perhaps scared you a little bit.

When is a time where you didn't know what to do, when you were operating at a level outside your pay grade (that's a metaphor for feeling a sense of overwhelm) — where you didn't have the answers, but you were forced to act? This could be a great way to show how you grew and changed, how you met the challenge and exceeded expectations — in many cases, your own. That could again offer more evidence of where you've been an achiever, just maybe in an area that doesn't come quite so naturally to you — where you've had to work harder to be a success.

To expand on it: Have you ever been in a situation when:

- You saw an opportunity, and you decided to go for it — but you didn't know how?
- You were faced with a challenge, and you didn't feel equipped?
- You were asked to do something without enough training?

We recommend presenting something positive, where it was YOU who took the initiative — where you were proactive. It shouldn't be a time where you were up against a wall and you had no choice but to act; those tend to not make great essays. An example of that passive story would be when you were laid off and you had to find a new job. This type of thing doesn't play so well because you had no other alternatives. Typically, the stuff that someone describes in a recovering-from-a-layoff story is the same stuff that anyone would do in those circumstances; it doesn't give us any new information about who you are as a person. If a story will be worth presenting in Essay 1 then it really needs to be operating in a different dimension than that.

Finding a story that talks about how you sought out a challenge or opportunity – or possibly that you were faced with your own limitations and you decided to change something about yourself – these stories could make for a great Sloan Essay 1. Just please refrain from using the phrase "comfort zone" in it or the MIT adcom reader will assume that you may have cribbed your topic from an essay submitted for last year's application, due to the identical language. Such a story will be one that depicts how you took action to change a situation; these stories are never passive.

Where have I improved the world?

As with the other categories, don't put yourself in too tight of a box when you first start to think about this – this "improve the world" thing could sound daunting. "I haven't improved the world, I'm just trying to make it through the day," you might think.

If you scale back the definition of "world" and make it "Where have you improved the lives of one or more people that you know?" then it should instantly suggest some ideas. Use that as your writing prompt for this exercise if you prefer. As with the other exercises, come up with two or three examples if you can. Impact and contribution are great ways to show achievement, and "impact" is obviously a specific question that the adcom is inquiring about in the recommendations piece.

There may be some overlap in how you think about this topic and the earlier one about "advancing a mission." If you nailed a great example on the prior list then you maybe don't need to worry about coming up with another one here, and vice versa. However, more topics to consider for inclusion in these various parts of your application are only going to help you throughout.

Got your lists done? Or at least started?

What you just did was analyze, and engage with, all the different components that are embedded in the prompt for MIT Sloan's Essay 1, and several of them required for Essay 2 as well.

Your job with Essay 1 is to answer the question based on the examples that you come up with – you need to make the case that you belong in their community, using evidence that shows how you have the traits that they say they value.

The raw material you've identified in those lists will take you more than halfway there. Now you need to analyze and filter the possible ideas that you've got.

You may find that going back over those same brainstormers again in a few days can be a very fruitful exercise – your brain may keep working at the problem while you're out doing other things, then when you turn your attention back to those questions at a future time, you may be surprised by the new ideas that come out. This is one reason why essay development takes time; sometimes the inspiration starts slowly before it really flows.

Once you have your lists after a couple of these brainstorming sessions, you're ready to move on to the next step.

Which Ones, and Where to Use Them?

So. Your Sloan app needs to be oozing with achievements. You just came up with lots of ideas. Which ones to present and where?

Essay 1 is how you establish your platform for the adcom reader. You don't have to cram everything in – but it should give them the key themes of your profile. We would rather you did not repeat yourself too much. Remember that your resume encapsulates your work history, and Essay 2 is going to talk about another couple examples of accomplishments, too. What you decide to include where and how you organize the information is up to you – we are not going to dictate a single strategy that everyone should use. Except that the content of your Essay 2 needs to be pretty much entirely focused on professional examples. If you have a strong story from your extracurricular activities, then that can certainly work for Essay 1 – if it's positioned appropriately. And all your stories need to be from the past three years.

You may want to go back over your lists now, to cull out any stories that are just too dated.

As you start to examine which story potentially belongs where, please remember that if every component of your app has the same stuff in it as the other parts, then you're not taking full advantage of the opportunity to present your complete self to the adcom. We offer this caution not only to warn you against repeating stories within your own two essays, but also to be aware of how many people end up using multiple examples that all sound the same. You want to have variety of experience, and variety of takeaway messages for your reader.

The don't-repeat-stuff doesn't extent to the resume. The resume should be all-encompassing. You must have stuff repeated there if it's elsewhere in the app; the resume should encapsulate it all. Everything in the essays and recommendations should also be on the resume, but the resume should be more than that, too. Some things on the resume will not also be featured in an essay or rec. Obviously the resume will go back further than the last three years. The essay stories cannot go back that far, and the examples your recommenders use in their two formal recommendations should also be focused on the more recent past. The resume covers everything.

The essay stories must be the biggest, most important things in your life. Again, don't cram. You have other application assets that will also convey who you are. This is quality, not quantity – but in the beginning, keep the funnel open so you can get more ideas to come.

Within the last three years: Is this a rule?

Short answer: Yes. It's part of the essay instructions. Take it as gospel.

During the idea generation step, you may have listed out some topics that you can't use in the essays, based on the three-year requirement – but they still might work somewhere else. The resume, for example. As long as the activity really belongs as part of your pitch for bschool.

Sidebar on "really belongs": Every year we get a handful of Brave Supplicants who still have the Eagle Scouts on their resumes – really?? Weren't you like 12 when you were a Scout?? OK, we get it, Scout for life, you're proud. If you're an active troop leader or whatever today, then sure it's relevant to an app and you could keep it – but otherwise, it seems to us at least, no, it should be deleted from your resume.

Same guideline with anything older than college. Please don't be so nostalgic. We advise against including anything from high school, anywhere in your app. (Some schools ask what high school you attended, so you obviously fill out that field in the online application; we're talking about referencing high school in other places.) OK, *maybe* if you were Valedictorian of your graduating high school class, you could slip that in somewhere – but we wouldn't. That's just old news. It would take up way too much space on the resume, which would then leave less room for you to talk about your recent awesomeness. We prefer to see you focus on stuff from when you were an actual adult.

Think about the types of things your mom is most proud of about you, the things that she brags about to her girlfriends.

All right, maybe that's not a great way to think about it. Maybe your mom still brags about you being an Eagle Scout.

How about, pretend you were going on a first date with someone you had a serious crush on. What might you want to tell that person about you, to share who you are and what you've done, in order to impress them? (OK maybe that example doesn't work so great either...)

The resume is the place where you *might* mention stuff like running a marathon or traveling to 15 countries. There's a bunch of candidates out there who've done those things and they usually don't work so great as essay topics, but maybe they're things you're proud of. We're not going to arbitrarily rule out any ideas sight-unseen; as with anything, it's up to you to make the judgment call on what's important, and then it depends on the execution in terms of how it comes across.

End sidebar on "really relevant."

You asked if you must limit your essays to stuff from the past three years, and EssaySnark says, "Yes." It is dangerous to disregard this.

This restriction on age of stories is another reason to apply in Round 1 — that three-year window is advancing each and every day! A quick note about that, actually: It's often better to talk about projects, initiatives, and contributions that are a little aged. In other words, we're not always convinced that something which happened yesterday gives the candidate the best opportunity for discussion. If you just had an experience recently, you haven't had time to integrate it into your life; any lessons-learned are still in the formation stage. There is no rule against using a story that happened this year, but generally we think ones that have "cured" a bit will give you more potential in what you can say about them.

If you've been working for at least two years (post-college), then it would be better if you didn't go back to your undergrad years for essay topics. Stick to post-graduation, and use something that has matured, so that there's a real story to tell.

An unfortunate reality

Since we're talking about this three-year restriction and whether it's a rule that you can break or not – and since we're about to truly dig into the essays themselves – we need to alert you about a very important critical-to-know please-be-aware-of-this fact about the MIT admissions team. This is an unpleasant fact, but it's one we have to state for you point blank.

They do not have their act together.

You may have already gathered from our negativity at the beginning of this guide and based on our posts about MIT admissions on the EssaySnark blahg and on Twitter that we are a little critical of this adcom. We've called them out for having inconsistent information available on their website (dammit, they even listed *the wrong phone number* for their admissions office on their blog on the day-of-deadline last year).

It's not just sloppiness. Here's why this matters.

Different admissions people reading the same application may be applying different standards to it.

We see evidence of this based on the different information that different MIT admissions people convey. The Internet chats that Sloan Admissions hosts on a regular basis are a minefield of conflicting information. The way their chats work is, you sign on, and then you log onto one of multiple chatrooms. They have one admissions person manning each of these individual chats, so that there are multiple chats going on simultaneously. They do this to make sure that they can get to all of your questions, since there are many more Brave Supplicants logging on to ask them questions than there are MIT people to answer them.

What happens in every single chat that we've ever participated in (which is many) is that the same question gets asked in different chat rooms, *and people get different answers.*

These are typically low-impact questions. One example from the early July 2014 chat was that one admissions person said that for reapplicants, the original application is not read when you reapply, while another admissions person said that it is.

We've had to ask for clarification on issues in the past. In the July 2013 chat, we asked them about how MIT calculates the years of pre-MBA work experience, since they said one thing on their website FAQ and another in a chat. The answer was that work experience is calculated up to the time of matriculation (so, next fall), which is how it works at every other school. But that's not what it had said elsewhere (the instructions were that work experience was calculated up to the time of application, so if you did it that way, you'd be up to one year short of how they actually want it totaled).

Here's a way worse example:

We had a client last year who we helped with some advice here and there, and he was working on his MIT apps on his own. He reported to us that he'd asked MIT admissions about the three-year requirement on their essays and they told him that it was not a mandatory requirement, that if he had a story he wanted to use that was outside this window, then it was completely fine to do so. We've heard them give that advice in the chats before — and we've also heard other admissions people say no, that it's three years, period.

Our advice has always been to be exceptionally conservative on this, but OK, if you feel that you have some story that is sooooooo unique and impactful, but older, then sure, it's your prerogative.

Well guess what? This Brave Supplicant not only didn't make it into MIT, but he wasn't even asked to interview. We don't honestly know what the problems were since we didn't see the essays — maybe he'd just failed to execute completely, and it had nothing to do with "coloring outside the lines" by using an older-than-three-years story.

But maybe that was it. Maybe his app was read by admissions people who feel that three years is a set-in-stone directive, who don't have this liberal interpretation of policies like the one who he spoke with.

Because we have experienced, multiple times, this phenomenon of MIT admissions people saying different things about how their policies work, then we are very very nervous of how applications might be received there.

If it's not in their formal FAQ, or even better, listed out as instructions on the application itself, then we say it doesn't count. It doesn't matter if you hear it in a chat, or you read it in one of those chat transcripts that they post, or you get it in a one-on-one conversation with an admissions person. All admissions evaluations are a subjective process — even MIT's, with their formalized assessment using standardized criteria that we spoke of earlier — and we're simply concerned that there's more variance at this place than we've experienced from other schools. They're not running a tight ship these days and it could impact you.

Essay 1: "The Mission"

> *The mission of the MIT Sloan School of Management is to develop principled, innovative leaders who improve the world and generate ideas that advance management practice. Discuss how you will contribute toward advancing the mission based on examples of past work and activities.* (500 words or less)

First, please spend some time figuring out what MIT means with this "mission" stuff. They're trying to get you to talk about their values and their culture, or at least to show them how you're the type of person who is a good fit to those values and culture. This is a common approach from schools like Berkeley-Haas and Duke in their essays too, so you might want to spend some time on the EssaySnark blahg reading up on the essay critiques we've done for those two schools questions in the past. Do a search for "defining principles" to find them on Haas, or view the blahg posts by category for the "essay critiques" section.

For MIT, you can also check out a few sections of their own website, though we don't find them to be the best articulators of their own meaning.

Just as an example, there's a page on mit.edu that talks about their "Core Values" yet the whole thing is just thinly-disguised marketing copy about what they think makes them so great. But you might want to read it anyway:

http://mitsloan.mit.edu/mba/program-components/core-values/

Slightly more useful might be the Dean's Statement which tries to communicate the type of school that they are:

http://mitsloan.mit.edu/mba/program-components/core-values/deans-statement

Finally, there may be some Values Statements lurking within the online application; the admissions team hasn't opened the 2014 app as of the time of this writing, but last year they did have some goodies on values buried deep within it. It's worth hunting around for those to see if you can find them.

If you have a story that maps to some of those sentiments, it can certainly be an effective way to tie your background into the school's "mission" - either overtly, by a direct reference to such things (which sometimes comes across as a little clumsy though) or indirectly, by simply emphasizing the qualities in yourself that reflect these traits that MIT is highlighting in these different places.

In terms of choosing the just-right stories to use and how to present yourself in this essay, here are some guidelines:

1. You can literally talk about anything from any part of your life, work or personal. For most people, both essays need to cover primarily professional stories, with perhaps some dabbling in extracurriculars for part of Essay 1. This is not set in stone; you are striving for topics that communicate the most they possibly can about you. It's up to you to determine where to pull the stories from for this first essay.

2. As already mentioned, you need to keep it recent; they state very clearly that you can't go back further than three years, and no, you really can't. No exceptions.

3. You should spend some time teasing apart what Sloan means with the different elements of the question.

The best bit of advice we can offer to help you get oriented to these two essays is, look for stories that, yes, fit the respective questions – *but look for ones that also are vehicles for you to present other good stuff.*

You want a multi-layered approach.

Here's an example: We said earlier that international experience is always useful to present to any adcom.

If you spent a month in Korea on a project, then do some brainstorming around your time there, to see if you can come up with a story that fits one of these essay questions that happened during your overseas assignment.

IMPORTANT: You should not pick a lame-o story for one of these essays only because it has an added dimension like international experience. If you don't have any examples of advancing a mission, or pushing the envelope, during that month in Korea, then drop it. It's not a valid strategy for you to deploy that in an essay. Instead, you can make sure that the Korea experience is highlighted appropriately on the resume – and maybe suggest that one of your recommenders discuss that assignment – but don't try to forcefeed the essay with elements that aren't going to work.

Another warning about no forcefeeding: We've already stated that leadership and contribution are both important traits that MIT is looking for. If you get through these exercises and don't feel like you have anything to talk about that shows you as a leader or a contributor – if you haven't really accomplished much yet – then consider putting this idea of an MBA to the side for now. There's no shame in putting bschool off for a year. You could go do more with your life and think about applying to MIT next year.

Your Most Significant Accomplishments

OK you're right – the question doesn't say anything about "accomplishments." That type of sentiment only comes in with the recommendation-essay.

But think about it: If you need to give examples of how you "advanced the mission" some time in the past – which is what they are asking for – then doesn't it indicate you "accomplished" something? Hopefully when you did your brainstorming, you identified examples where the accomplishment part is clear. If not then now might be a time to revisit your list of topics, to see if you can easily articulate what the "accomplishment" was in each one.

Then you need to figure out which might be the best to use for this essay.

Candidate Examples for Essay 1

Here's an imprecise and inexact broad-strokes recommendation of what accomplishments might qualify for essay 1. This first essay needs to include one or more of each type listed below, in any combination, with a minimum of one example from the first category:

1. Your absolute best, biggest, most impressive, most impactful professional achievement

2. An accomplishment that showcases how you've been involved in the community (volunteering, nonprofit, etc.)

3. A personal accomplishment, maybe something with team sports, or music, or overcoming a personal challenge such as significant weight loss (running a marathon *might* qualify, but frankly, lots and lots of people talk about running marathons).

If you have two work-related accomplishments, then they must be different projects – ones that are clearly dissimilar. Even better would be if they're pulled from two totally separate jobs in different companies. Sometimes people use two accomplishments that are really really alike — like a PE guy independently sourcing and closing two different deals, an analyst looking at the cost structures of two different companies. It would probably be better to choose just one of those, and then find other stories to tell to round out your profile. Even if the deals are of two totally different investments in different industries with really different challenges in pulling them together, they're likely going to sound too similar on the face of it, and it's important to bring variety to this essay if you can.

The main litmus test for which accomplishments you choose: **Each needs to be something that you personally took action to achieve.** It's fine and great if they are team-based achievements, either sports or on the job or whatever, but it needs to be YOUR accomplishment, that you worked towards, that you pulled off.

Ideally you'll have four cherry accomplishments that meet these guidelines – two as examples to use in Essay 1, and two to use as the basis for Essay 2.

As we've been hammering home, you need to look at what what you want the adcom to know about you. You want them to see a balanced picture. You want to show them multiple sides of yourself, your accomplishments from different parts of your life. And, obviously, you want this story, which is hopefully about an accomplishment, to capture something IMPORTANT. The "important" can either be that the project you were on and the accomplishment you achieved was significant. Or, the "important" can be how you portray your own skills and strengths in the essay. The way you describe what went down in this situation is what the adcom will come to know you from. They'll be forming impressions of who you are and how you deal with people and maybe teamwork stuff and all sorts of other things based on the details you offer on the page.

Note that this is a non-trivial task! Just selecting the right story is fraught with challenges. Then, figuring out *how to present it* – and then layering in these very sophisticated angles on top – all of this will require multiple drafts. You are unlikely to get this down in just one sitting. You should plan to write and rewrite this.

So the stories you choose to tell should not just be a generic time when you had to, for example, get someone over to your way of thinking. It should be set within a larger context of significance; it should be a time that the stakes were high.

Remember that we're talking about REAL-WORLD ACTUAL EVENTS in these essays. The MIT people often lament a common mistake in their essays, that people talk about hypotheticals. This is not at all what your task is. You need to be down and dirty in the literal things that happened – to the degree that you can do a "he said/she said" type exchange in the story if that's appropriate. (Or, "he said/I said" more like.) Just don't go so far into the weeds that your reader gets lost. Again, it needs to be balanced.

What must be in Essay 1

We're focusing on accomplishments since that's going to be how you back up your argument. But that's not the entirety of the essay. It's critically important that the essay directly answer the question.

You cannot simply include a bunch of examples of stuff – that's only a start. Your essay must have a premise from which the argument is made.

While MIT is asking for accomplishments in this essay, the QUESTION is asking about "advancing the mission." If the accomplishments that you present don't fit that question then it will be an #essayfail.

Here are two requirements for this essay:

1. You really really should open the essay with a statement of what you're going to say about how you "advanced the mission" in some context. It's up to you to interpret their meaning and apply it to your life. We strongly feel that language about "the mission" needs to be somewhere in the introduction of the essay; that's how you set the stage for the stories that will come thereafter.

2. You must have a focus on why you want to go to MIT through some angle or emphasis. This can come later on, in the conclusion, or you can include it somehow in your opening, but it must be there somewhere.

We wish we didn't have to spell things out quite so clearly however we know that there's a risk, with all our talk about accomplishments and examples, that some people will simply upchuck three examples of stuff they did into a draft and call it a day. That is not an essay. An essay has a POINT – and in the case of an MBA admissions essay, it must ANSWER THE QUESTION.

This question is asking you to state why you belong at MIT – based on who MIT is and what they're about. And they're asking it using specific language and terminology that's important.

If what you write seems to have no bearing whatsoever on the question that MIT is asking, it will go straight to the reject pile.

A key reason that the Sloan adcom has developed such a challenging question is to see how you handle it – and another is to make sure that you wrote the essay from scratch, for them. There is no way you can repurpose an essay for any other school and use it for Sloan.

How to write Essay 1

Here's the instructions that the MIT essays came with last year – this is definitely still helpful this year too:

> "For each essay,
>
> 1. please provide a brief overview of the situation
> 2. followed by a detailed description of your response."

In the "your response" part, they ask that you "please describe in detail what you thought, felt, said, and did."

There's two parts. First, quickly set up the situation. Since you're (ideally) you're using multiple examples in Essay 1, then the setup for each section cannot require more than a few sentences. Then move into an explanation of what happened and how you handled it. A conclusion at the end will wrap things up – and the whole thing should open with a introductory line or two to set the stage for the theme of the essay itself.

A common problem that we often see? People spend a bunch of time at the beginning of the essay with this high-level introductory mumbo jumbo. This is not necessary and it's quite the waste of space. That being said, it's often difficult to write a first draft (or a fifth) without having that type of sentence at the beginning. You need to ease yourself into your topic, and writing *around* the essay is what most people do to get acclimated to what they plan to say in the nitty-gritty of it. It's fine to have that in your early draft but as you move through the revision process, the opening is one of the first places to look for opportunities to trim back and pare down.

Instead of saying "Here's what I'm going to tell you" as your first sentences, you should start the essay by JUST TELLING THEM. You definitely do need an intro sentence that sets the stage – establishes the theme of your topic, directly answers the question about "the mission", something like that – but then your stories should speak for themselves. You don't need to *explain* a story before you tell it; you need to tell the story and let the reader understand what it means. (You should still have some takeaway messages which are often explicit but those would come later, in the conclusion, when you connect the dots between everything that you're saying.)

So a structure for Essay 1 can be something like:

1. Answer the question re: how you would advance the mission (this is your thesis)
2. Tell story #1 (this is your first bit of evidence that your thesis is sound)
3. Explicitly link story #1 to your thesis and/or to Sloan
4. Tell story #2
5. Explicitly link story #2 to your thesis and/or to Sloan
6. Conclusion w/ takeaway messages and more Sloan stuff

That's about all you have space for. The bulk of it needs to be on you/your stories.

Do that exactly and you'll be batting a thousand with this first essay.

Finally: Each of your Sloan essays needs to be a single page total, of not more than 500 words. They don't count words, but they can tell when people get creative with font size and margin in an attempt to squeeze more on the page. This essay cannot spill to a second page or you are doing something wrong.

Essay 2: Your Recommendation (Of Yourself)

This is just another "greatest accomplishment" essay question in disguise.

But boy oh boy, is this a disguise.

On the one hand, you can just rattle your way down the list of questions that the adcom has posed for you – keeping in mind that the adcom is asking your recommenders to answer the exact-same questions about you, too. You don't want too much of what you say to sound too much like what your recommenders say.

The obvious advice for this?

Because you're writing your own recommendation letter, as Essay 2, then that means *you totally cannot write your other recommendation letters, for your recommenders to submit.*

We've always been crystal clear in the advice that we offer to Brave Supplicants about this point. It is flat-out unethical to write your own recommendations for business school. No matter how busy your boss is, or how much easier it seems for you just to draft something up for him to submit for you, you absolutely cannot under any circumstances whatsoever even think about doing that for Sloan.

(You really truly should not do it for any schools, but you won't be able to do it here even if you wanted to.)

Why not? Because adcoms can tell when you write your own recommendations – there are often telltale signs just in terms of word choice and writing style – and those will be near-impossible for you to hide if you attempt to do a formal rec draft for your boss, at the same time as you're having to write this self-recommendation for Essay 2.

Some of the business school media outlets covered this new "essay" when it was released, so you might want to check out these articles if you have not seen them:

- http://www.businessweek.com/articles/2014-06-13/new-mit-sloan-application-requirements-ask-students-to-write-their-own-recommendation-letters
- http://www.businessweek.com/articles/2014-06-25/business-school-admissions-offices-devise-creative-new-essay-questions-each-year

All of that is not even the biggest hurdle you'll have with this (and we didn't expect that you were even thinking of writing your own formal recommendations anyway, we just had to get all that out of the way as a starting point).

The biggest challenge you will face with this recommendation essay is, how do you actually position it? How do you write about yourself?

- Do you write it in the third person, as if you were someone else, talking about you? "I recommend John Smith because..."

- Or do you write it as yourself, acknowledging in the presentation that that's the stance you've taken? "If I were Sally Jones, my most recent supervisor, then I would say this about me..."

Both of these options are clumsy and difficult to do with a natural voice – especially since Sally Jones, your most recent supervisor, most likely is actually submitting a recommendation. Either way you go stylistically, you're setting yourself up for writing headaches. We think that it will be slightly easier if you were to simply assume the persona of your boss, Sally Jones, in which case you can do it like this:

> **"My name is Sally Jones, and I'm a portfolio manager at Acme Investments. John Smith has worked for me as an analyst since August 2010. John stands out from other analysts I've worked with because..."**

Your challenge with this is that *even though you're you, and you know everything there is to know about you, you must limit the material that you present in Sloan Essay 2 to stuff that your boss knows about you.*

That means, you cannot use this essay to talk about college stuff, if you have been working at all and you're writing it from the perspective of your manager. Sally just won't know anything about your college experience.

You also probably shouldn't bother talking about why you want to go to MIT here. Is there anything in the series of questions that asks about that? Would your boss even know the real reasons why you are interested in business school? Maybe she does – but not all bosses will, and it doesn't seem like the most natural of topics for you to be covering in your boss-impersonation task of writing this essay.

We recommend making an outline of exactly what you will say in response to each of the questions that Sloan is asking you to cover, in the order that they've listed them. As a reminder, those questions are:

> 1. How long and in what capacity have you known the applicant?
> 2. How does the applicant stand out from others in a similar capacity?
> 3. Please give an example of the applicant's impact on a person, group, or organization.
> 4. Please give a representative example of how the applicant interacts with other people.
> 5. Which of the applicant's personal or professional characteristics would you change?
> 6. Please tell us anything else you think we should know about this applicant. (750 words or less)

The best way to answer these questions? Especially questions 2, 3, and 4? By using those examples of accomplishment that you defined for yourself with all the brainstorming you did. While it's fine to use reasonably short-answer statements in response to question 1, the others need more content, and probably a bit more context.

A Snarky Caveat

> If you try to cover every single point we're raising below, you'll have a 3,000-word essay. The best approach is to find two stories that communicate how you are a leader who's ahead of her peers. Focus on telling those well in this essay. But write it as a recommendation.

We're going to break down the six questions separately, so you can see what might go into a solid answer for each. You should read through the entire set before starting in on the first one, to get a lay-of-the-land view and see if you can determine which of your stories might work best to cover multiple angles at once.

Here we go.

1. *How long and in what capacity have you known the applicant?*

This is the simplest and most straightforward of the set. What to include:

- Your boss's name, and his/her title or role, and the name of the company where you work. If for some reason you don't currently work with this person (the only reason we can think of for that is if you were recently laid off) then explain the circumstances of that. Or, another exception: If the person you worked for at this company for the longest time was recently reassigned or they quit, and you have a brand-new boss for whom you've only worked for six months or less, then it would make sense to write this recommendation from the perspective of the previous manager. Just be clear on why that person is writing it ("I am writing this recommendation for John even though he stopped working for me in July because I had a long relationship with him and he felt I would be the best person to speak to his abilities." Or something.).

- If you work for a very small company, then you could use this opportunity to educate your adcom reader on what the company is/does. Very briefly state the industry or segment.

- Your title or role at the time you were hired, and your current title if you've been promoted. If it's not clear what you do from the title, then explain it (again, briefly).

- Your boss's professional relationship to you (e.g., "direct supervisor" etc.)

- How long you have worked directly with your boss . This should include duration and recency, as well as how long you've worked in your company. Example: "Mary worked for me from November 2011 until she was promoted to our Audit team in May 2013" or "Ryan was my analyst on three projects last year; each one lasted two months."

All of these elements can be conveyed in a sentence or two. This first question does not need a very involved answer.

One caution is warranted here:

A Snarky Caveat

> The instructions say to write from the perspective of your current boss. It might be acceptable to say "My colleagues report XYZ about this candidate" but you should not combine anecdotes and examples of your performance from multiple jobs at various different companies.

2. How does the applicant stand out from others in a similar capacity?

All schools want to admit overachievers who are ahead of their peers. That's what you need to demonstrate here. This question would benefit from use of a quick story but it's not mandatory, as long as you are able to answer it with concrete details of some sort. What you might include:

- How have you performed in comparison to others of equal training and experience? This is specifically what the school cares most about. Be sure to identify the peer group to whom your boss would compare you – e.g., "John stands out from the dozens of first-year analysts in my 10-year career because of his …"

- You could then name a handful of specific strengths or personal qualities that your boss values about you – and try to give a reason, or some insight into why your boss would say this. "I am impressed about John because of his ability to …" These are just ideas for how you might phrase things; please explore and expand upon this in your own words.

- When you name your strengths (from your boss's perspective), give a specific instance when you showed that quality. Don't say "She is very dedicated." That is a generic statement. Instead, give some particulars; demonstrate how you are that way. Talk about the time last year working on the project for your biggest client when you performed above the call of duty. Go into details on the actions you took. That's the best way to share how you're strong in this area.

Tip: Dig up your most recent performance review, and check out what your boss has named as your strong suits. You need to be consistent with whatever she is going to say, too – she's answering the same questions as you are when she submits her own recommendation, so these things better sync up! Just avoid nondescript terms such as "dependable." If you want to convey that you are dependable, think of an example to illustrate that, and relate it to the Admissions Board. However, don't be afraid to name a strength such as "her sense of humor" if it's what your boss values about you.

Some additional ideas that you might want to discuss for this part:

- Have you been promoted ahead of schedule? If so, what did you do to earn that? This would be a totally appropriate thing to mention here.

- What have clients said about you to your boss? What about your boss's boss, and others above her in your organization?

- If you have a job title that's below what you feel is appropriate, you could comment on why. Does your company maintain a flat organization? Is there a freeze on promotions? This is a great opportunity to inform MIT if you feel there is a discrepancy between your strong performance and what's reflected in your title.

- The best way to answer this question is to tell a story. Identify one or two examples where you went above and beyond the expected, where you outdid yourself and truly impressed your boss or her superiors. This can come from any aspect of your working relationship. Describe a specific example of an achievement or contribution that you made, that reveals or demonstrates one or two key strengths. You must have AT LEAST ONE such example in this essay, preferably two. It's more important to have a vivid example to illustrate why you have answered in a specific way. THESE EXAMPLES ARE THE MOST IMPORTANT PART OF YOUR ESSAY.

- Quantified results are especially helpful. If you can characterize your achievements based on impact to the team, group, company, or client, those can be extremely valuable.

- Remember that this is asking for insights about yourself in comparison to the peer group. If you are is an analyst and all analysts at your firm are equally good with building models, then building models is not a strength for you. If you build the best models on the team, then it is – but man oh man you need to be careful how you write about this. Yes, you need to toot your own horn, but you're still writing about yourself, even if it's in disguise. If you come across too strong with your self-praise then it just isn't going to look good – especially if your real recommenders don't come through with equally effusive language. Be conservative. Show some humility. The best approach is to stick to the facts, and use concrete examples to make your point.

Actions speak the loudest. The school will appreciate hearing about literally the things that you did to create results.

3. Please give an example of the applicant's impact on a person, group, or organization.

This question needs a story to illustrate your answer.

- Identify a time that you made a specific contribution, and tell the story of what you did. This should go beyond a time when you made a positive impression on someone; "impact" should be more definitive than that. Where did you move the needle on a project? Where did you come up with an important solution to a problem, or bring people together in a new way, or otherwise catalyze change? You should have at least one or two ideas from the brainstorming session you did earlier. Results reported from clients can be especially illustrative.

- When you explain this story, it can be useful to explain the "before" state, and then tell the actions that you took and what the results were. As with the previous question, quantified results are extremely useful. If you can define your strengths based on impact to your team, group, company, or client, those can be extremely valuable.

Even though we're offering less guidance here on what to say, that doesn't mean that this question is less important. We mostly covered the standard tricks for conveying "impact" in the prior section; all of that applies equally here as well. This one is probably the most important of the entire set of questions that you're answering. You should have a heavy-hitter story here; it should be obvious what the "impact" was without requiring too much explanation. The connection between the actions that you took, and the outcomes with this "impact", should convey this very easily and not require any type of interpretation for your reader. It should be self-evident why this is an important instance that you're sharing, and it should also be very clear why YOUR BOSS would be sharing it with the adcom.

In fact, this is a key question where there might be overlap between what you say and what your boss says. Our best suggestion for how to handle that is, when you discuss the possible topics that your boss will be covering in her recommendation, avoid going into too much detail. In your conversation about the contents of the recommendations, you can suggest the topic – "The ABC project was pretty important, right?" – and let her acknowledge that. Don't dive into the details of how or why it was important. You can then present your perspective of why this example is impactful and relevant, and how it made a contribution to your company, while at the same time, the adcom will get a very useful third-party perspective on the same story, given by your boss, with her views and insights on its importance to her and her job. This is the best way to handle this requirement that both of you end up featuring the same or similar examples, yet those examples should each be unique and separate in how they are being presented in these two documents to the adcom. Resist the urge to get too involved with your boss on what she might want to discuss on the specifics of this project. Simply reinforce to her that she needs to focus on tangible evidence of "impact" as a way to sufficiently answer the question.

4. Please give a representative example of how the applicant interacts with other people.

This one also requires a story (or at least, a clear example, per the instructions) however this needs to be much less involved than the example(s) you may be using for the previous two questions. In this case, the adcom wants an example that shows how you typically act. Don't use some outlier example of you being an incredible hero here, it won't be believable. You need to offer an example of you "in action" that shows your standard way of being.

Some ideas for what that might be:

- Can you relate a time when you were effective in reaching agreement, finding consensus, bringing others together, getting a mutual goal accomplished, or accomplishing some other project or task that required sensitivity, compassion, diplomacy, or similar "soft" skills? Please be specific.

- An alternative example would be anything related to negotiations, team-building, mentoring, managing up or down, dealing with seniors, dealing with clients, on-boarding new hires, etc.

- Or, is there simply a time when you were kind? That shows how you are generally kind? (If you're not generally kind – or if you're coming from a sharp-elbowed place like a bulge bracket Wall Street bank – then maybe this isn't the best story to use. Remember, "representative example.")

These are suggestions to get you thinking about topics; don't feel limited by them. This question is important, but we do not feel that it's the most important one of the bunch. You definitely should not skip it but you also don't need to dedicate undue amounts of your limited essay real estate to covering this one. The trick will be in getting yourself in the mind of your boss in how you present your answer. It doesn't work to say "John is very collaborative" and stop there; you'll need to offer some significant detail(s) to back up such a claim, otherwise it just will come across as a puffpiece. This is the type of question that will be more difficult for you to answer in this "personification mode" that the adcom is forcing you into with this stilted recommendation-essay exercise.

5. Which of the applicant's personal or professional characteristics would you change?

For the "real" recommendations, this is one of the most important questions that MIT is asking. For you, it's important as a means to show self-awareness and humility (and emotional intelligence) however it's also SUCH a difficult question for you to handle.

You're writing it from the perspective of someone else – what would THEY want you to change – but you're the one writing it. No matter what you say, it's going to sound odd.

"I think John should change this."

If that's the case, and since you're John, then shucks, why don't you change it?!?

Sitting there as you, if you're aware of what your limitations are and that others don't like them, then why on earth would you still have those limitations?

Sure, everyone has weaknesses, and we're often asked to do self-assessments for our annual employee reviews and such. But don't those always feel so contrived and fake? It's great to take inventory of our problems and list out all the ways we could be better. Yet the way you're having to answer this question in this recommendation-essay is just so artificial and awkward.

What we can suggest most of all is don't get coy and try to use a strength disguised as a weakness. An authentic, genuine answer to this question is best. Many people sugarcoat this answer which is not helpful for anybody. You do not need to pretend that you, as the applicant, are perfect. Having some honesty in your answer will take you far.

What to consider for your response:

- Ideally, you will name one or two weaknesses. Please be specific. You might want to refer to a formal employee evaluation for ideas. If possible, choose areas of development that you have discussed with your boss, and that you are actively working to improve; you can then mention that in your answer. Everyone has areas for improvement. Where do you struggle? What is a project that your boss might hesitate to give to you – or you would be nervous about accepting – based on your knowledge of your own limitations? Or, where did you royally screw something up in the past, based on your short-sightedness or inability to deliver in some capacity? Mistake or failure stories are often quite useful in communicating something "real". One of these topics might be good to present.

- Please avoid naming things that are really strengths in disguise; e.g., do not say that "John is a perfectionist and sometimes turns in reports late because he takes extra time to proofread them." The areas for development that you name need to be real. Be honest. The school wants to get a holistic view of who you are – and your answer needs to at least not completely contradict the stuff that your recommenders will give (this is one case where probably you don't want verbatim overlap in what you say, versus what they say). Everyone has blind spots and things they are not as strong at. That's what this question is asking for. The most common answers are things like, "Joe tries to do too much" or "Mary cares too much about her clients." These are not useful responses.

- Please DO NOT say "Lauren has never had an opportunity to manage a team" or "Jason has not worked overseas before." These are not areas for development; these are simply things you have not done before. This type of answer is useless to the school.

- Some weaknesses or personal shortcomings may be self-descriptive and require little explanation; others would benefit from providing an example to illustrate your point. The best stories to use are ones where you were able to fix the problem and redeem yourself yourself in this end. If you include this detail then it will be more useful to the MIT admissions team.

- Ending this section with a positive statement is preferred. You could touch on how you are improving, or taken steps to fix this deficiency.

6. Please tell us anything else you think we should know about this applicant.

This one is tricky. Is the adcom asking you, the applicant, to address anything else they should know? For example, is this the place for you to talk about your low GPA in college, like you would do in an optional essay?

No, and no. This would be, if *your boss* would want to convey something specific about you and she hadn't been able to fit it in through the five main questions, then she gets an open-ended opportunity here to fill in those gaps and add additional context or explanation. But for you the applicant, we can't imagine much that you'd need to provide here. If you have something that you really need to convey to the adcom that is specific to your professional environment and/or the skills that you've been deploying in your current job, then sure – but we just aren't seeing much that would qualify for this.

No matter what, you should wrap everything up with a statement to the positive – particular depending on how you have answered the fifth question about stuff you need to improve. You need to bring your reader's mind from that negative-ish place, into something positive that pulls the entire thing together. Remember that the instructions say that you are recommending yourself to this program. Use a statement like that at the end of it; make sure it comes off as a positive endorsement.

How to write Essay 2

For all of these questions in the recommendation-essay, you'll have to weigh out all the different possible stories you could tell and see which one communicates the most about you. There's a number of ways you can go with presenting your content for this "recommendation." MIT accepts actual *letters* written by people in support of their candidates, provided that the letter covers all the angles that they're asking about in these six questions. Or, more common, and what we would suggest you deploy, is for recommenders to do more of a Q&A format, where it looks more like a report than a letter. What we don't suggest is writing it as an essay, where you have an opening, then a couple paragraphs that answer the questions in block form, then a conclusion at the end. That format doesn't seem to match up to what they have asked with this write-a-rec thing.

If you do it as the Q&A style, then feel free to format it with question numbers and bold subtitles or however you want to do it. We think that it helps to include the questions on the page (sort of like a FAQ is laid out) so that the adcom can see what you're explicitly responding to for each one. Or, if you feel that the main story you want to present appropriately responds to multiple questions being asked, then you need not break it out into separate sections, since that layout doesn't lend itself to having one example be used for multiple purposes. A "real" recommendation letter doesn't exist too much in the world of business these days, so it's up to your own discretion, to some extent, in terms of how you design the look-and-feel of your response.

Important: This recommendation letter is a great opportunity for you to fill in any gaps in skillset or readiness that the adcom may be worried about from the basic stats of your profile. For example, if you're coming from a non-traditional background where you have very little quant experience, then you could use this "recommendation" to include some examples from the workplace where you've deployed your analytical skills in some important ways. This is how you can create for a multidimensional answer, where each essay is working for you on multiple levels simultaneously. It's even better (or perhaps preferable) for your real recommenders to cover those angles, too, since a third-party account of your strengths in such areas will obviously go further. But don't overlook the opportunities that are available to you in what you choose to present, and how.

Unabashed plug: We have a bunch of resources to help you make sure you've got your messaging right – including an Essay Ideas & Outlines App Accelerator, which allows you to submit your proposed essay topics for vetting before you start writing your drafts. These two MIT essays consist of telling stories, it's going to be important that you uncover the essence of your story beyond the mere facts and events that went down in the circumstances of your accomplishment and setback.

Before you get too far with Essays 1 and 2

Before you start writing the essays, step back and ask yourself, *What do I want the takeaway message to be?*

What are you trying to communicate about yourself with these four examples from your life? Sometimes you need to get through a draft or two and then ask this question.

You'll need to look at the messaging you're creating. What do you want the adcom to know about you as a result of this combination of stories? They will be forming impressions of you based on what you say and how you say it. The details matter a lot. This is how they'll be able to score your app on those competency scales.

You should be able to review your draft and extract a specific word or two about each essay, a couple of adjectives that are the key ideas of the content you're presenting. Add them up. Are these qualities that you think make you into a qualified MIT MBA candidate? If someone knows just these main stories about you — that you did this one thing, and this other thing, and this is why your boss finds you valuable— what is the net-net? What do you think a complete stranger would assume to be true about the type of person you are, based on just those facts?

You may need to tweak it a little — or a lot — before you find the right combination.

And while you go through the process of thinking up ideas and evaluating them and scratching them off the list – don't scratch them off the list permanently.

Snarky Strategy #6

Keep building this list of your key accomplishments, strengths, and qualities. You may need it later.

If you are indeed ready for a top bschool then you will find yourself coming up with plenty of possible essay topics as you work through the exercise of what to present. It is not an easy task to identify which are the strongest. But don't worry about it too much, because even if you can't fit an important story into your essays, and even if your references to it on your resume and the application dataset seem too abbreviated to convey its importance, and even if you can't get one of your recommenders to talk about it – you still may have a chance to present it to the Admissions Board later.

That's because the MIT adcom specifically will want to hear new stories when you go to interview with them. The interviewer will have read your application. They will ask you a bunch more questions that start out "Tell me about a time that..." Having an inventory of stuff you've done in the past will only help you not be a deer in headlights when these questions get served across the table to you.

A full discussion of interview prep is out of scope for this *Guide* (we wrote a whole separate book on that) though we will touch on the basics later on, since MIT does things differently. For now, you should be capturing your ideas on paper, and not discarding them. Maintain a running list. You never know how you may need that later on.

Optional Answer

This essay is an invitation.

Normally EssaySnark is adamant that the optional essay not be written. However, MIT has snuck in a little change with the "optional answer" this year. This is still a completely optional submission – but they've opened this up significantly. A few years ago, this question was very specific – you were asked to only write about your "academic background" here and it could only be 250 words. At the time, it was called the "supplemental essay" – you'll note that it's not even an "essay" anymore. That's all different now. This "optional" thing is completely open-ended and unstructured.

Here's a post from the MIT Admissions blog – with a video – about where the Admissions Board is coming from on the optional information section.

http://mitsloanadmissions.com/2013/09/20/optional-essay/

This submission can include any weaknesses or extenuating circumstances that you need them to know about – low GPA in college, gaps on your resume, that sort of thing. Those are standard topics for an optional essay. If you have those issues to explain, then write a traditional essay – keep it short – and use the Optional Answer for that.

If your profile is decently solid with no glitches or blips that need explaining, then that's where the opportunity comes in. You can present something personal to the adcom with the Optional Answer, preferably in a non-written format.

How do you decide which to do and how?

Develop your entire application strategy first. Look back over your lists and examine if there's anything you absolutely need to tell the adcom about that cannot be covered elsewhere. Weigh it out on an importance scale. If there's something critical that you need to convey, then write about it (250 words max is our recommendation). If there's something else that's distinctive about you – no, not that you were in the Eagle Scouts, something else perhaps – then this could be the place to slip it in.

You might particularly want to take advantage of any multimedia presentation that you may have developed for another school. Chicago Booth wants a PowerPoint. NYU has the Personal Expression option. If you're applying to any of those schools and you've already created that application asset – and you're convinced that it's additive, and not redundant, to what you've already covered in your base MIT application – then sure, why not? Sloan has asked for it. If it's critical info that you don't have elsewhere, then go for it.

Just remember that in prior years, they couldn't accept Flash because they're viewing apps on iPads; unclear if that limitation still applies today but we think it does. And all submissions need to be posted somewhere on the Internet and then you provide the URL in your application. They have stated that using Dropbox for files, or "any link that is set to expire", has caused problems. We heard the adcom suggest using Google Docs, so maybe that's the way to go instead. YouTube is the obvious solution for a video. There may be other sites to host things, such as one of those PowerPoint hosting sites like Slideshare. There are plenty of other file formats and media to consider using so please don't feel that you're limited to only one of these types of submissions. The world is wide open to you. It just needs to be served on the Internet.

One point to that: You cannot have a password on your file; it must be open for viewing by anyone on the Internet with the URL. These technical issues need to be sorted out early.

Also, when you post your submission, then be sure to test the URL from multiple other machines. Try to view it from your phone, just as an example, and ask your mom or your brother to retrieve it from their computers. Make sure that others can get to it, too; sometimes we are able to view things that we post because we're logged on, but others will be blocked from viewing them even with the same URL.

You do not HAVE to do this Optional Answer – and if you do do it, doesn't HAVE to be a fancy video or presentation, it can be a straight-up essay that you copy/paste into the field. We caution against frivolous submissions. Don't submit something because you think everyone else is doing it and you believe you'll appear lesser-than if you do not have something in this section. Be honest with yourself. Anything you include must increase the adcom's understanding of who you are – in a positive way. If this is too hastily thrown-together, if it seems sloppy or unfinished or rushed, then it may be better to skip it.

Or, if you have time to build out a submission and you do a bang-up job on it, whatever it may be, then great – and if you don't, then also great, you've completely satisfied the requirements and you should be confident that you're submitting a whole package even without this.

Resume

Every bschool (except the ISB and INSEAD) wants a resume uploaded as part of your application. We explained earlier that you will need to put some work into it – the version you have on hand from the last time you were in the job market is likely insufficient for these purposes.

This is another area where MIT has provided explicit instructions on their website. They even have a template that you can use from their application. You are not required to use their template, but you can. If your resume is well-designed, clean, clear, and complete as you now have it, then go with that and don't think you must re-create the wheel. There is no advantage to submitting yours using their template if what you already have is professional and appropriate.

EssaySnark has posted on the blahg about resumes in the past so you might want to start there. A standard resume is important, nothing too creative – you want it to be easy to scan. Fonts and margins should be reasonably sized. You don't want job descriptions on the resume – you want statements of achievement and contributions. The education section should be at the bottom, unless you're coming straight to Sloan from an academic institution.

You need to do this rework regardless of which bschool you're applying to. You will redo the resume just once and use that new-and-improved version for every application; you need not update it for each school. MIT calls out the resume as a critical part of the entire application – what other school does that? You need to take this seriously.

Resume services are available from EssaySnark if you want input on what you've put together. (We won't write a resume for you, we will respond to what you've developed.) Please make all the updates to your resume that you possibly can on your own first, before sending it over for your review – don't send your old one over and expect us to tell you everything that needs to change (we don't respond well to Lazy Supplicants).

The resume is pretty important, especially with the ever-shrinking essay real estate in today's bschool applications. The process of updating your resume is best tackled after you have your platform established. We typically recommend holding off on that until the essays are at draft 2 stage if possible e – at that point you should have more clarity on the stories you're presenting and how the resume may need to reinforce them.

Questions on the resume tend to be easy – you might even have luck tweeting them to us if you want.

The MIT Interview

The MIT interview process is another way that they're different. The MIT interview is actually near-identical to the Harvard experience, and NYU does them in a similar way too (as does LBS except that there, it's alumni doing the interviews). So MIT isn't completely unique, but these are a small subset of the overall population of business schools in the world. You need to prepare for your interview according to how the school conducts this part of the process.

Unlike Harvard, MIT has no set pattern or schedule for when interview invitations come out. It can be grueling to go through the post-submission wait. Candidates might even be invited to interview *on decision release day* – way out in January, when the Rd 1 app was submitted in October. At that point, you will have likely given up on MIT and moved on emotionally.

Applicants get rather obsessive with trying to read meaning into when an interview invitation comes through. They spend countless hours on the Internet forums, asking questions of other candidates who've been invited, about what geography they're in and when they submitted their apps, trying to deduce if they are next in line for an invite based on their location on the planet or whether they were "early" or "late" in getting their application in. You should resist the mania that goes into this. There's nothing that can be interpreted from the timing of an interview invite, and even if there were, there's nothing you could do with that information.

Once you hit the Submit button on your application, you lose all control over the process. You may want to get familiar with the Serenity Prayer – surely you've heard it? "Lord, grant me the serenity to ..."

If you don't know it, look it up.

After submission, everything that the adcom does with your app is in the category of "things I cannot change."

If you're the type who wants to know the numbers regardless, here's some data about MIT:

- Applications have increased at Sloan nearly every year for the past five years. Most recently they've been at about 4,500 – up from around 3,000 within the decade. Pretty impressive.

- They invite around 800 candidates to interview total across the admissions season, half in each round

- They accept half of those interviewed

Obviously, getting the invite is a very good sign.

The main reason most candidates blow it at the interview are when their essays don't match up to how they present in person (i.e., someone else wrote the essays), and/or they come across as arrogant. Or they're just not prepared.

There's no excuse for not being prepared.

Why?

> ***Because MIT will give you an interview guide when they send you the invite.***

Yes, they are this awesome about how they treat their candidates.

It's OK to be nervous for your interview — in fact, it's to be expected. The best way to minimize the jitters is to do plenty of prep work ahead of time (again, you can check out the EssaySnark blahg for help on interview prep).

Logistics

The MIT admissions team travels to specific cities around the world to conduct interviews, or you can travel to Cambridge and interview on campus. If you can pull that trip off, you should do so — but it's not technically necessary. (Note that if you apply to LGO, you *must* travel to campus for your interview; don't apply if you can't do this.)

Interviews at MIT are invitation-only, and they are conducted by members of the admissions team themselves. This is different than how it works at many schools, where the adcoms tend to recruit the alumni and current students to do the bulk of the interviewing. MIT doesn't do it that way. They feel (and EssaySnark tends to agree) that the best way to get a sense of the applicants is to have the same small set of people have these interactions with those applicants. They have a much better sense of who they are admitting than another school can, just based on the fact that it's this small team making the decisions after actually meeting with the candidates themselves.

The main difference with a MIT interview as opposed to most other schools is that it's an open interview. The person you meet with will have read your entire application and will have questions prepared for you that are specific to you. These cannot be predicted in a vacuum (though EssaySnark can help you prep for this experience if you'd like some guidance; see the website for options). You can expect the MIT interviewer to have studied your application. Then, they will have prepared a list of what are called *behavioral questions* — which are essentially the same model as the ones you answered in the essays.

We walk you through how to prep for an open interview in the *Interviewing Guide* and we do interview prep through Skype, too, in case you're interested in getting some professional help for this.

A Snarky Caveat

> Try not to reuse stories from your essays. Bring new examples to the interview that show how awesome you are.

Again, we wrote a whole book on how to prepare, so you may want to pick that up to assist in your process.

What to Do Next

As we've said over and over, this *Guide* is a mere starting point. Keep doing the research and talking to people. Get to know the differences embodied by the MIT experience. See how you can articulate those. Revise, rewrite, practice. It'll all come together when you take it step by step.

Remember that another reason for you to be highlighting your accomplishments in these essays is that MIT does not offer any need-based financial aid; all is done through merit evaluation on the application. They even have a perfectly-named Achievement Fellowship Award that you may want to read about here:

http://mitsloanadmissions.com/2014/05/23/achievement-fellowships-awarded/

That should provide even more evidence of how important achievements are at this school, and give you a bit more motivation to do a bang-up job of expressing yourself through them in these essays this year.

Want more tips? Swing by the EssaySnark blahg at essaysnark.com (or find EssaySnark on Twitter) to ask about strategy, or if you have questions on how we can help you out, drop the team an email at gethelpnow@essaysnark.com to inquire about our specialized MBA admissions consulting services for MIT, Harvard, Wharton, LBS, and all the other top bschools in the world.

FOLLOW ESSAYSNARK ON TWITTER!

www.ingramcontent.com/pod-product-compliance
Lightning Source LLC
Chambersburg PA
CBHW081917180426
43199CB00036B/2816